Norman Lockhart Walker

Scottish church history

Norman Lockhart Walker

Scottish church history

ISBN/EAN: 9783337235086

Printed in Europe, USA, Canada, Australia, Japan

Cover: Foto ©ninafisch / pixelio.de

More available books at **www.hansebooks.com**

HANDBOOKS

FOR

BIBLE CLASSES.

EDITED BY

REV. MARCUS DODS, D.D.,

AND

REV. ALEXANDER WHYTE, D.D.

WALKER'S SCOTTISH CHURCH HISTORY.

EDINBURGH:
T. & T. CLARK, 38 GEORGE STREET.
1882.

PRINTED BY MORRISON AND GIBB,

FOR

T. & T. CLARK, EDINBURGH.

LONDON, . .	. HAMILTON, ADAMS, AND CO.
DUBLIN,	. GEORGE HERBERT.
NEW YORK,	. SCRIBNER AND WELFORD.

BY

REV. NORMAN L. WALKER,

DYSART.

EDINBURGH:
T. & T. CLARK, 38 GEORGE STREET.
1882.

CONTENTS.

CHAP.		PAGE
I.	THE CHURCH OF THE FIRST CENTURIES,	1
II.	HOW SCOTLAND CAME TO BE ROMANIZED,	12
III.	WHAT LED TO A REVOLT,	18
IV.	THE REFORMATION,	26
V.	PRESBYTERY AND PRELACY,	40
VI.	UNDER THE COMMONWEALTH,	62
VII.	THE PERSECUTING TIMES,	70
VIII.	THE REVOLUTION ESTABLISHMENT,	87
IX.	THE SECESSIONS,	101
X.	THE ERA OF MODERATISM,	111
XI.	THE EVANGELICAL REVIVAL,	127
XII.	CONFLICT AND DISRUPTION,	142

SCOTTISH CHURCH HISTORY.

CHAPTER I.

THE CHURCH OF THE FIRST CENTURIES.

WHEN Agricola invaded Scotland, toward the close of the first century, he found the country black with forests. For that reason alone we may conclude that the population was small and scattered. The natives mustered, indeed, in considerable numbers when there were battles to fight, but the proportion of combatants to a whole people was immensely greater in those days than it is now, and the size of the armies they were able to bring into the field gives little idea either of the strength of the tribes which the Romans had to encounter, or of the extent to which these tribes were allied to one another. That there was then no united nation is absolutely certain. The country was loosely occupied by different communities or clans, each with its separate chieftain. And it is more than probable that these communities did not all come originally from the same stock. The country is so situated that it can be reached from all quarters,—from England, from Ireland, from Scandinavia, from the European Continent,—and we see no reason for assuming that that mingling of races which appears as taking place during the historic period had never occurred in earlier times. Whether the ancient Caledonii were all painted, and whether that was what secured for them, to begin with, the common name of PICTI, is still a debated point among the antiquaries. But supposing it to be settled that such was the case, we should still be as much in the dark as ever with regard to the original homes of the inhabitants. All that we certainly know is, that there are unmistakable memorials in our soil, in our language, and in our mythology—first, of an aboriginal population; and, secondly, of successive visits paid to our shores by Norsemen, Romans, Teutons, and Gaels. The Roman invasion must have been of special value to the country in several ways, and very notably in this way, that it helped to make us a nation. Long after they retired, indeed, the land was still divided into three kingdoms. But when they came there were, we have no doubt, as many different tribes as the white man found among the Indians of North America. A common interest brought those together. The exigencies of the defence placed in the foreground their ablest men. And in course of time the SCOTS, whoever they were (some say they came from Ireland, others from Scythia, others that they were merely one of the aboriginal 'painted' clans), got finally the upper hand, and gave their name to the whole country.

We do not stay to discuss the question, how Christianity was first introduced into Scotland. It is a point which can never be settled, and which really is not of very much consequence. There are three things, however, which come out quite clearly in such records as we have, viz.—(1) That the process of conversion was (at least after a time) tribal rather than individual; (2) That, as a result, the religion of the country retained for long a large admixture of practical paganism; and (3) That in the conduct of the missionary enterprises of the time, certain individual men took conspicuous and memorable parts. Now-a-days it does not follow that when any great man changes his creed his dependants change with him. Each of us claims a right to judge for himself. But time was when the clans did not presume to differ from their chiefs, and then the conquest of one individual implied the almost certain submission of a multitude. Such conversions, however, were necessarily superficial, and there occur in the history from time to time, plain enough indications that whole districts relapsed into

THE CHURCH OF THE FIRST CENTURIES. 3

heathenism and needed to be reconverted. The outstanding missionaries of these days were St. Rule (rather a shadowy figure), St. Ninian, Bishop Palladius, St. Patrick, St. Serf, St. Mungo, and St. Columba. What we read about them is as follows :—

1. **St. Regulus.**—St. Rule (or St. Regulus) was, they say, an Eastern monk to whom was committed the charge of finding a grave for the bones of St. Andrew. For this he searched in vain along the shores of the Mediterranean, but happily found it on the East Coast of Scotland. Landing at what is now (and hence) called St. Andrews, he converted the Picts of the neighbourhood to Christianity, and founded a church, of which the tower still standing and bearing his name is the memorial. The date of St. Rule's visit is 369. It is impossible to say how much of truth there is in the legend, but that it has some foundation in fact, we cannot doubt. Perhaps it is here that we are to seek for the origin of the tradition, that the first to plant the Cross among us were not Romans, but Oriental Christians.

2. **St. Ninian.**—When St. Rule was landing in the Bay of St. Andrews, St. Ninian was but a boy of nine. He was a very precocious youth, however, and as he very early became convinced that the Christians around him (he was of English parentage) did not properly understand the Scriptures, he resolved to go to Rome for more light. The story bears suspicious marks of having been written at a date when 'going to Rome for light' had grown commoner than it could have been in the fourth century, but we must take it as we find it. It goes on to tell that the young inquirer remained for several years in the imperial city, that having been instructed sufficiently he was ordained [by the Pope] as a missionary bishop to his countrymen, that on his way home he visited St. Martin of Tours, the father of Monachism in Western Europe, and that having received from him some lessons in ecclesiastical architecture, he proceeded at once, when he had landed in Galloway, to erect a stone church, which from the

whiteness of its walls came to be known as the *Candida Casa*, or the White House. This was in 400, twenty-three years before the Romans withdrew from Great Britain. From this date Whithorn became a centre of Christian influence, the conversion of the Southern Picts being generally ascribed to the labours of St. Ninian and his coadjutors. Tradition credits the saint with the performance of many miracles. We need not recount them, but we do not need Bede or any other chronicler to convince us that he did a really wonderful work in his day, because he has left his mark permanently on the country. No fewer than five-and-twenty churches and chapels, scattered all over the land from the Shetlands to the Mull of Galloway, are known to have borne his name.

3. **St. Palladius.**—About thirty years after St. Ninian had built his White House another ambassador arrived from Rome. This was Palladius, who is described as having been sent in 430 by Pope Celestinus to be the first Bishop of the Scots. His commission is awkwardly worded. At least Episcopalians think so. For it seems to imply, on the one hand, that the Scots were already Christians, and, on the other, that they had organized themselves into a church without a bishop. They get rid of the difficulty by supposing that he was sent not to originate a Scottish Episcopate, but to put the copestone on it, by becoming the 'Primus Episcopus,'—the first bishop in point of rank,—in plain words, *the Primate*. This is a far-fetched, not to say grotesque, explanation. The truth is, that for many centuries there was no such thing as Prelacy in the Scottish Church. Palladius either came as a missionary to teach the Scots the way of truth more perfectly (for by this time heresies—Pelagianism, for example—had begun to spread), or he came as an emissary, to secure, on the side of Rome as against Constantinople, the countenance of the Caledonian Christians in the struggle which had commenced for supremacy. If the latter was his object, he failed in it. If the former, he met probably with some success, for tradition

THE CHURCH OF THE FIRST CENTURIES. 5

describes him as settled at Fordoun, in the Mearns, where he gathered around him a company of admiring disciples. And the remembrance of him has been preserved in that neighbourhood to this day. A well was named after him, and the anniversary of his birth and death was observed. His name, indeed, has been abbreviated, so that it is now hardly recognisable in the colloquialism into which it has passed, and the holy day of the saint has been diverted from its original purpose. But there seems no reason to doubt that 'Paldy's Well' and 'Paldy's Fair' commemorate the services of the great Roman missioner.

4. St. Patrick.—Contemporary with Palladius, although accident made him an Irish saint, was St. Patrick. He was born on the banks of the Clyde, his father being a deacon and his grandfather a presbyter. The fact is interesting as showing that at this date (the middle of the fifth century) there was no such thing known as the celibacy of the clergy. St. Patrick in his youth fell into bad hands, and was carried captive into Ireland. There a great change came over him, which led to his devoting himself to the work of the ministry. In place, however, of returning to the land of his birth, he began at once to preach in the Green Isle, and hence it is that a Scottish Christian occupies the most conspicuous place in the Irish calendar. It is not improbable that the Scotland of his day felt also to some extent the influence of a man whose eminence must have been unquestionable. The two countries were near enough to know something about each other's proceedings, and Scottish Christianity could not but receive an impulse from sympathy with the labours of so great a compatriot.

5. St. Serf.—Among the disciples of Palladius were two men, traces of whose labours still remain. One of these was Ternan, whose name lingers in the north in connection with Banchory; the other was Servanus, or, as he is more familiarly called, St. Serf. St. Serf appears to have been the principal of a theological

institution at Culross. It is indeed in connection with him that we first meet in Scotland with that kind of agency with which the story of Iona and of the Culdees has made us so familiar. There were no parishes or parochial clergy in these days. Christianity was propagated and kept alive by itinerant missionaries. And to provide and maintain these there were formed centres after the model of the ancient schools of the prophets. Unless there was another Servanus of the same type, which seems hardly likely, St. Serf transferred his college in course of time from Culross to an island on Lochleven, which still bears his name. There his light shone far and near, and continued to shine after his death, for the Lochleven institution developed into a Culdee establishment, which flourished till the twelfth century.

6. **St. Kentigern.**—While St. Serf was still at Culross, a skiff was one day driven ashore there bearing a young and beautiful lady. She was the daughter of a Pictish king, had been accused of incontinency, and had in consequence been cast away to perish on the sea. The princess was, however, more sinned against than sinning. After a time she gave birth to a son, who became famous in the Church under the name of St. Kentigern. The infant was brought to the saint to receive his blessing, and he, struck with its beauty, and having perhaps some premonitions of its future eminence, took it into his arms and spoke to it endearingly, calling it, in the language of the country, 'Mochohe! Mochohe!' that is, 'My darling! My darling!' The affection so early displayed continued. The boy attended the mission school at Culross, and was much taken notice of by the principal, who got into the habit of calling him not by his own long name of Kentigern, but by the pet name of Munghu! My dear one. And so we come to be introduced to St. Mungo, who in course of time was called to the ministry of Strathclyde, and who took up his abode in what was then a small town in that district, but which has since developed into the great city of Glasgow. St. Mungo is said to have been born in the year 514, and to have

lived to a very great age. He wrought many miracles, like St. Ninian, the greatest of which were certainly those which issued in the diffusion of Christianity throughout a wide region in the west of Scotland.

7. **St. Columba.**—Some six years after the boat containing the Pictish princess had been cast ashore at Culross, there was born in County Donegal, Ireland, one who was to repay the Scotch for the loss of St. Patrick. This was Columba. Being of royal blood, he was, though he became an ecclesiastic, not able to keep clear of the political troubles of his time. His own country became unsafe for him, and, accompanied by twelve followers, he crossed the sea and settled down in the island of Iona. There he founded a religious community, which appears to have done more toward the diffusion of Christianity throughout Scotland and the north of England than any other agency of which history speaks. The institution was in a sense a monastery, that is, a number of men lived together in it whose sole link of connection was their common interest in religion. But it differed widely from the Papal establishment of the same name, inasmuch as the members were bound by no vows of celibacy, and the main object they had in combining together was not the carrying on of perpetual local services, but that of spreading abroad the knowledge of the gospel wherever they could find a field. It was, in short, a missionary institute suited to the times, and it proved a well of life to the whole country in an age when the territorial system of sustaining ordinances was as yet unknown. Columba died in 597, leaving behind him an extraordinary reputation. His biographer says: 'His name has not only become illustrious throughout our own Scotia and Britain, but has also reached Spain and Gaul, and penetrated into Italy beyond the Alps, and even to the city of Rome itself.' In any case, he has left his mark very distinctly upon his own adopted country. There are at least fifty-three places in Scotland where his work is commemorated in connec-

tion with wells or churches that had been dedicated to him. The ruins which are still visible at Iona are the remains of buildings which Columba never saw, for the architecture of his day was of a very much humbler description. But they speak for the importance of the institutions which he founded, and which were continued through many subsequent generations; and we may still say with Dr. Samuel Johnson, 'That man is little to be envied whose patriotism would not gain force upon the plains of Marathon, or whose piety would not grow warmer amid the ruins of Iona.'

8. **Other Missionaries.**—As we look back into that time, other figures, more or less shadowy, flit across our line of vision. Some of these have left such provokingly distinct footprints on the country, that we cannot doubt about their having been important personages in their day. But their personality has for ever fled, and not even a legend remains to help us to a conjecture as to their history. Who can tell us, for example, anything about the doings of St. Maelrubna; and yet his name haunts to this day some of the most beautiful spots in the Scottish Highlands. He was an Irishman, like Columba, but he came to Scotland when he was twenty-five, and settled at Applecross. After a ministry of fifty-one years (as we are told), during which he lived in the odour of sanctity, he died in his chosen Ross-shire, and was buried on an island in Loch Maree. We know little more of Baithean, Kenneth, or Donnan, although memorials of all the three are to be found in the topography of Scotland. All that seems clear is this, that here and there, and from time to time, men of mark were raised up to preserve and extend the light of Christianity, and that these invariably acted on the one plan of having a common missionary centre with a number of outlying stations.

9. **The Culdees.**—Dark, however, as this period is, it is light as compared with that which follows. For five hundred years—

from the seventh century to the twelfth—the annals of the Church mysteriously disappear, and we can only guess at what happened during this long interval by noticing what was the condition of things before it began and when it ended. The era on which the cloud rests is that of the Culdees. Dr. Hill Burton, who is, one might say, almost contemptuously fair in his discussion of ecclesiastical questions, shows a curious animus against these remarkable communities. On the whole, he inclines to think that 'Culdee' was a nickname used in the days of Queen Margaret to distinguish those who refused to assent to the 'reforms' which she instituted in the Church. But he scouts the idea of their being the successors of the Columbites, and holds that although they may have been 'bad Papists,' they were certainly far enough from being 'Protestant evangelicals.' If Dr. Burton had given conclusive reasons for his beliefs in this connection, we should, of course, have felt obliged to give way before so high an authority. But he does not reason; he simply asserts. And to us no reading of the times seems more natural than that which assumes the continuance through the five dark centuries of very much the same forms of religion as prevailed beforehand at Whithorn, at Culross, at Iona, at Abernethy, at Applecross, at Lochleven, at Dunkeld, and at St. Andrews. That the Church of this time did not preserve all the best features of the primitive period is admitted. Rich endowments came to be bestowed upon some of the Culdee establishments, and secular interests were bound up with them. It is a suspicious circumstance, too, that as the centuries go on, 'saints' grow fewer, that is, there are fewer outstanding men distinguished for their religious earnestness. But all the information we have about the Scottish Church before the cloud fell, during its continuance, and after it lifted, distinctly countenances the impression that it was throughout one and the same organization with that which we are made familiar with in the history of Columba.

It is not quite certain what the word 'Culdee' means. Some

trace it to a Latin origin, and suppose that the Culdees were
'Cultores Dei'—worshippers of God. A more likely interpretation is suggested by an account given of the disciples
of St. Kentigern. They are described as living apart and
piously in small dwellings of their own, and as being called
popularly CALLEDEI, which, says Dr. M'Lauchlan, is just the
Celtic *Cuiltich*, or *Men of the Recess*. The first form of the
National Church was that of a congeries of mission centres with
dependencies. These were, to begin with, strictly spiritual and
evangelistic. But as the early fervour decayed, they tended to
degenerate, and it was probably easy enough to transform some
of them into Roman abbeys. What took place, however, in the
twelfth century, was obviously a conflict between the old order of
things and the new. Under the direction of St. Margaret and
her sons, strenuous efforts were made to bring the Scottish
Church into conformity with that of England and of Rome, and
the Culdees were, ecclesiastically, the patriotic and conservative party. It is possibly true, as has been affirmed, that the
'soundness' of the later Culdees has been exaggerated. We
can hardly think that they exactly corresponded to the modern
'Protestant evangelicals.' At the same time, it is clearly no
fond fancy which pictures the primitive Church of Scotland as
maintaining for centuries a sturdy independence, and as
asserting opinions of its own in the face of all the threaten-
ings and cajolements which came from the Vatican. It
held its own, for example, in the controversies which arose
very early about the Tonsure and the keeping of Easter. It
refused to recognise the Roman supremacy, to which England
soon submitted. It accepted Diocesan Episcopacy only after
the immigration of the Saxons. And there are many things
which warrant the statement, that the Bible did not cease
very soon to be studied, or to be the supreme rule of
faith.

    1. *What is known about the early state of Scotland?*
    2. *How was the gospel first successfully propagated in it?*

3. Name the men who appear to have been concerned in the founding of the Church.
4. What memorial is there of St. Rule?
5. In what ways is St. Ninian still remembered?
6. For what purpose is it said that Palladius came from Rome?
7. Where was St. Patrick born?
8. How does he come to be the patron saint of Ireland?
9. With what districts is St. Serf associated?
10. Which of these early missionaries gave his name to Glasgow?
11. Relate his history.
12. Which is the most famous of them all?
13. Of what country was he a native?
14. Wherein did the establishment at Iona differ from a Popish monastery?
15. Give the names of any other famous men in those days.
16. Who were the Culdees?

CHAPTER II.

HOW SCOTLAND CAME TO BE ROMANIZED.

THE Norman Conquest, which took place in 1066, did not change the face of England alone. It told influentially on Scotland also. It started a tide of emigration which continued to flow northward for many a year after the battle of Hastings. The Anglo-Saxons did not like their new masters, and such large numbers of them crossed the border, that the very speech of the Scottish Lowlands became affected by their presence. If William the Bastard had not come over from Normandy in the end of the eleventh century, and begun a new page in the history of England, it is more than likely that the whole of the Scottish people would to this day have been speaking Gaelic.

1. **St. Margaret.**—Among those who sought shelter in the north were the dethroned royal family of England. The story goes that Edgar, the young Saxon Pretender, landed with his mother and his two sisters at a spot near Queensferry, which is still called in memory of the incident *St. Margaret's Hope*. From this spot the little party journeyed on foot toward Dunfermline, where the Court then was—a pilgrimage of which there is also a memorial in the shape of a wayside resting-place, called *St. Margaret's Stone*. Malcolm Canmore was at that time king of Scotland, and he received the fugitives with open arms, spending afterwards no little blood and treasure in the endeavour to restore to them their inheritance. That, however, does not at present concern us. What we have to note as of more importance, is that Malcolm fell in love with one of the young princesses, and

persuaded her to become his Queen. That event was far-reaching in its consequences. Margaret, although she was not formally canonized for centuries after her death, was a more genuine *saint* than most of those whose names fill the Roman Calendar. Her religion had a sad admixture in it of the superstitions of the time, and she did much mischief in her too successful efforts to propagate it ; but there can be no question as to the depth of her personal piety, or as to the sincerity of her desire to glorify God according to her light. One conclusive proof of the force and purity of her personal character is seen in the impression she produced on her own household. Her rough husband was devoted to her, and would frequently kiss her books, though he could read none of them ; while of her three sons, all of whom in succession ascended the throne, each seemed more anxious than the other to carry out, in matters of religion, their mother's wishes.

2. **Her Reforms.**—The state of things in the Scottish Church did not please the Saxon princess who had become queen of Scotland, and under her active superintendence there began that process of assimilation to English ecclesiastical ways which in the hands of her youngest son David issued in the establishment of 'Catholic unity.' In some respects, indeed, she wrought a real reformation. The law of marriage had been so relaxed that unions were taking place within prohibited degrees, and she insisted on its being restored to its integrity. Sabbath-breaking also had become common, and she succeeded in persuading the Scots that they ought not to continue the ordinary work of the week on the Lord's Day. And it may certainly be added, that by the force of her own example and the stir she made about religious matters generally, she elevated the character of the Court, and diffused a new spirit of earnestness throughout the country. But though the ancient Church unquestionably needed a revival, it is more than doubtful whether she set the breeze blowing in the right direction. Her controversies with the

clergy, which were frequent, were not always about points of supreme importance. The subject of one, for example, was as to the day on which Lent should begin. But the whole drift of her policy was to break down the distinctions which she found existing, and bring about conformity to the Roman standard, and her sons would perhaps not have succeeded so well in their open efforts if the way had not so far been cleared for them by their saintly mother. She died in 1093.

3. **Her Three Sons.**—Of the three sons of Margaret, David is the one to whom Rome is most indebted. Edgar's reign was short and, except in its stormy morning, uneventful. Alexander inherited the fierce spirit of his father, and was overbearing to ordinary men, but he would do anything for the clergy; and it was in his day that the process began of enriching the Church at the expense of the Crown. David, however, was his mother's son— gentle, pious, superstitious, freehanded, with an entire devotion to the cause which he believed to be that of God. It is interesting to remember that he died in the attitude of prayer.

It was unfortunate for Scotland that in his earlier days David was led to spend so much of his time in English circles. He married a daughter of the Earl of Northumberland, and through her came into possession of the barony of Huntingdon. This made him an English noble, and in that character he attended the English Court, and made the acquaintance of those Norman gentlemen of whom so many afterwards found their way to the palace of Dunfermline. When his brother died he returned to his native country to receive the crown, but he returned Anglicized and Romanized, with the same determination which in later years possessed Charles II. to mould the Church of Scotland after the glittering model which he had seen on the other side of the Border.

Unhappily the Culdee Church was not made of the stuff which afterwards appeared in the Covenanters. It had become spiritually dead, and palpable abuses of various kinds existed in it.

Many of its institutions, for example, had been made rich by the pious liberality of its members, but in not a few instances the endowments had been appropriated by the children of churchmen for their own use—only a fraction being devoted to strictly ecclesiastical purposes. There did remain, probably, something of the primitive faith and practice. The celibacy of the clergy, for one thing, was not insisted on. But there had ceased to be any pith or enthusiasm in the system, and the King was allowed to have his own way, with scarcely any opposition.

4. **The Sair Saint.**—What David did was simply to reproduce in Scotland the identical Church system which he had found in England. 'He wrought a change in ecclesiastical affairs,' says Dr. Cunningham, 'almost as great as that which was subsequently accomplished by Knox. He in effect built up that which Knox, when it was in a state of decay, pulled down. He drove out the now antiquated Culdees, and introduced prelates and priests : Knox cast out the prelates and priests, and brought in Protestant preachers. The proceedings of the one as well as of the other are frequently spoken of as a Church reform. It is certain that David remodelled our whole ecclesiastical polity. He originated the hierarchy, and gave it its splendour. Nearly the half of our bishoprics, and the abbeys of Kelso, Holyrood, Melrose, Newbattle, Cambuskenneth, Kinloss, Dryburgh, and Jedburgh, were founded by his munificence. He brought several orders both of the Augustinian and Benedictine monks into our country, transplanting them from their great monasteries of France and England; and it was under his favour that the Templars and Knights of St. John took up their residence at Southesk and Torphichen.'

A king who could accomplish all this in one generation must have been no ordinary man ; and if, as has been suggested, these ecclesiastical changes were only parts of a great scheme of State reform,—if David's hope was to refine and elevate the tastes of his nobles and the character of his country through the Church,

—we must concede to him a very high place indeed among the wide-thinking statesmen of the world. The plan could not possibly be a perfect success because of the imperfection of the instrument he had to use. But it was a grand conception, and full justice perhaps has not been done to him for entertaining it. Men from all lands are still visiting the wonderful abbeys of Dryburgh and Melrose. These creations of architectural genius continue to contribute to the education of the nineteenth century. And although our Scottish Solomon, King James, shook his head over the extravagance, and in the midst of his own impecuniosity ruefully complained that his pious predecessor had been 'a sair saunct to the Croon,' it would be gross ingratitude on the part of those of us who have not suffered through David's munificence, to withhold from him so far the tribute of our admiration.

5. **The Church in the Dark Age.**—It is not necessary to linger over the history of the Papal Church in Scotland. With its general features everybody is acquainted. Romanism here developed itself in very much the same way as it has done elsewhere, and if any one wants to realize the condition of Scotland in the thirteenth, fourteenth, and fifteenth centuries, he has but to look at Spain in the present day.

But there are two things which may be referred to in passing as having a bearing on the after attitude of Scotland in ecclesiastical matters. I call them two things, but in reality they may be traced up to one and the same source. Very soon after the establishment of the hierarchy in Scotland, claims were put forward on behalf of the English Church to exercise spiritual authority over its Scottish sister. This raised the question of the autonomy and independence of the Scottish Church, and in connection with the battles that were fought about it, the country was twice placed under the ban of Papal excommunication. The curse seems to have been submitted to with considerable equanimity. But a sorer trouble came when Edward I. attempted to destroy the political independence of North Britain, and bring the whole island under his heel. How much there is of the legendary in the story of Sir William Wallace it would be difficult to tell, but there seems no reason to doubt that if it had not been for the gallant stand made by him, Scotland would have settled down, like Ireland, into the position of a conquered province, with the spirit of the people chafed or broken, and its whole subsequent history complexioned and directed by influences from abroad. The peaceful union of the Crowns, which was brought about in course of time, has on the whole issued in satisfactory results to both countries; but in various periods we have been forced to remember that England is the larger and more influential half of the Empire, and our struggles for political and ecclesiastical independence have not been without their good effects in preserving for us some of the healthiest of our national characteristics.

1. *What effect had the Norman Conquest on Scotland?*
2. *To what one important event did it lead?*
3. *What was the character of Queen Margaret?*
4. *What good and evil did she do in the Scottish Church?*
5. *Which of her three sons most resembled her?*
6. *Where did he receive much of his training?*
7. *What was the consequence?*
8. *Has he, in any other ways, left his mark upon the country?*
9. *Describe his character.*
10. *Into what condition was the Church subsequently brought?*
11. *What encroachments were attempted on Scottish independence in Church and State?*
12. *To whom, among others, are we indebted for fighting our battles and preserving us from the fate of Ireland?*

CHAPTER III.

WHAT LED TO A REVOLT.

FOR two hundred and fifty years after the death of David—that is, from 1153 to the beginning of the fifteenth century—the Church of Rome had in Scotland unchallenged possession of the field. From the latter date, however, breezes began to blow from several quarters threatening its prolonged supremacy. One of these breezes sprang out of the very grossness of the Church's corruptions, producing as it did in the popular mind a deepening feeling of indignation and disgust. A second came from what was a notable feature of the time, the spread throughout Europe of a higher general intelligence. And a third was caused by the opening up to the people of the contents of the Bible.

1. **The Need of Reformation.**—That the Scottish Church of the fifteenth and sixteenth centuries needed some kind of reformation is frankly admitted by Papists themselves. It is not merely true that there then existed an ecclesiastical establishment, teaching for doctrines the commandments of men. What history tells us is this, that an institution which was intended for the promotion of godliness was altogether diverted from its purpose, and made to subserve instead the worst ends of worldly men.

The picture which Dr. M'Crie gives of the period is a very frightful one, but the trustworthiness of the biographer of Knox as a historian is well established, and we cannot therefore do better than quote what he says upon the subject.

'The corruptions,' he remarks, 'by which the Christian religion was universally depraved before the Reformation had grown to a greater height in Scotland than in any other nation within the pale of the Western Church. Superstition and religious imposture, in their grossest forms, gained an easy admission among a rude and ignorant people. By means of these the clergy attained to an exorbitant degree of opulence and power, which were accompanied, as they always have been, with the corruption of their order, and of the whole system of religion. The full half of the wealth of the nation belonged to the clergy, and the greater part of this was in the hands of a few individuals, who had the command of the whole body. Avarice, ambition, and the love of secular pomp reigned among the superior orders. Bishops and abbots rivalled the first nobility in magnificence, and preceded them in honours; they were privy councillors and lords of session, as well as of Parliament, and had long engrossed the principal offices of State. A vacant bishopric or abbacy called forth powerful competitors, who contended for it as for a principality or petty kingdom; it was obtained by similar arts, and not unfrequently taken possession of by the same weapons. Inferior benefices were openly put to sale, or bestowed on the illiterate and unworthy minions of courtiers or dice-players, strolling bards, and the bastards of bishops. . . . The lives of the clergy, exempted from secular jurisdiction, and corrupted by wealth and idleness, were become a scandal to religion and an outrage on decency. While they professed chastity, and prohibited, under the severest penalties, any of the ecclesiastical orders from contracting lawful wedlock, the bishops set an example of the most shameless profligacy before the inferior clergy. . . . Through the blind devotion and munificence of prince and nobles, monasteries, those nurseries of superstition and idleness, had greatly multiplied in the nation, and though they had universally degenerated, and were notoriously become the haunts of lewdness and debauchery, it was deemed impious and sacrilegious to reduce their number, abridge their privileges, or alienate their funds. The kingdom swarmed with ignorant, idle, luxurious monks, who, like locusts, devoured the fruits of the earth, and filled the air with pestilential infections. . . . The ignorance of the clergy respecting religion was as gross as the dissoluteness of their morals. Even bishops were not ashamed to confess that they were unacquainted with the canon of their own faith, and had never read any part of the Sacred Scriptures, except what they met with in their missals. Under such pastors the people perished for lack of knowledge. That Book which was able to make them wise unto salvation, and intended to be equally accessible to Jew and Greek, barbarian and Scythian, bond and free, was locked up from them, and the use of it in their own tongue prohibited under the heaviest penalties. The religious service was mumbled over in a dead language, which many of the priests did not understand, and some of them could scarcely read; and the greatest care was taken to prevent even catechisms, composed and approved by the clergy, from coming into the hands of the laity. . . . Of the doctrine of Christianity almost nothing remained but the name. . . . It is difficult for us to conceive how empty, ridiculous, and wretched those harangues were which the priests delivered for sermons.'

Dr. M'Crie adds: ' The beds of the dying were besieged, and their last moments disturbed by avaricious priests, who laboured to extort bequests to themselves or to the Church. Not satisfied with exacting tithes from the living, a demand was made upon the dead. No sooner had a poor husbandman breathed his last than the rapacious vicar came and carried off his corpse-present, which he repeated as often as death visited the family. Ecclesiastical censures were fulminated against those who were reluctant in making these payments, or who showed themselves disobedient to the clergy; and for a little money they were prostituted on the most trifling occasions. Divine service was neglected; the churches were deserted (especially after the light of the Reformation had discovered abuses, and pointed out a more excellent way), so that except on a few festival days the places of worship in many parts of the country served only as sanctuaries for malefactors, places of traffic, and resorts of pastime.'

We may safely allow ourselves to believe that all the priests were not like those described above, and that even in the darkest days there were some parishes in which a certain amount of light was suffered to shine. But if, on the whole, things were at all as M'Crie paints them, we can scarcely wonder that there should have come a revolt. The story goes that a precentor, who was discreet enough to hold his tongue while awake, once betrayed the state of his feelings when dreaming. Unfortunately for himself he had a habit of talking in his sleep, and he narrowly escaped having the honours of martyrdom thrust upon him, through his one night emphatically denouncing the priests as 'a greedy pack.' A good many are known to have been of the opinion of this honest precentor. The grumbling went on in private long before it found articulate expression, and the Church no more occupied the place it had done in earlier days, when the escapades of the monks became the subjects of bitter jests among the people, and the manners of the clergy were lampooned in satirical verses by the wits of the Court.

2. The Intellectual Awakening.—What helped to deepen the dissatisfaction with which the corruptions of the Church were viewed, was the intellectual awakening which took place concurrently over the whole of Europe. Toward this, some of the Scottish clergy themselves directly contributed. Among these was Henry Wardlaw, Bishop of St. Andrews, to whose exertions that ancient city is indebted for the establishment of its University in 1413. In 1450, the University of Glasgow was instituted, also through the intervention of the bishop of the diocese. Previously to these dates, there were youths who gave themselves to study, and for them some provision existed in the monasteries. But if any one wanted to excel, there was nothing for it but to seek some seat of learning abroad, and few comparatively could afford the means to do that. A great step was taken then

when home colleges were provided. One result must have been a marked increase in the number of educated men; and the Church thus unwittingly let light in upon the repellent spectacle of its own abuses. But it was not only the cultured classes, as we now call them, who felt the impulses of the new era. The very same year which saw the founding of Glasgow University saw also the invention of printing. Four-and-twenty years later, Caxton was at his press in England. And although it was not till 1508 that the first book was printed in Scotland, yet here, as elsewhere, the influence of the revival of letters was by and by experienced, and the nation rendered less and less disposed to tolerate the extravagances at which, in its ignorance, it had winked.

3. **Translation of the Bible.**—The Reformation, however, would never have taken place if it had not been for yet another cause. This was the diffusion of a knowledge of what is contained in the Bible. Wickliff died in 1384, so that before then the whole of the Scriptures had been translated into English. Of the translation thus made, many manuscript copies are said to be still extant, and we may therefore assume that the Book was very widely circulated in the age in which it appeared. The effects produced by the perusal of it were most marked. God blessed it to the conversion of not a few individual souls, and to the religious awakening of many communities.

Among those who were deeply stirred by it were some among the clergy. These 'poor priests,' as they came to be called, could not remain silent after they had received a divine message to deliver, and they began to preach, rivalling, as was said at the time, the mendicant friars in their zeal, or, as we might perhaps say now, acting as missionary evangelists. One such preacher, John Reseby by name, wandered across the border telling the Scottish people about the new gospel which he had learnt directly from the Word. But he had passed into a region where the darkness was as yet too dense to receive the light;

and the venturesome Wickliffite was (in 1408) arrested and burnt.

The same fate overtook, twenty years later (in 1432), another evangelist from a more distant country. Wickliffism had spread over the Continent, and the truth which it contained had touched the hearts of two men in Bohemia—John Huss and Jerome of Prague. The Council of Constance, which met in 1414, did its best to suppress 'the plague' by committing its most prominent propagators to the flames. But this method of stamping out the gospel has never been found to be perfectly successful. Persecution, for one thing, usually scatters the fire; and in this fact probably we are to seek the explanation of how a Bohemian physician—Paul Craw by name—came over to Scotland and settled in St. Andrews. The foreign doctor meant perhaps to confine himself to his profession, but his heart burned within him, and he could not be silent. Very soon, therefore, the town began to ring with his teaching. He denied transubstantiation and purgatory and the efficacy of absolution, and insisted that the people ought to have the Bible in their own tongue. We can well imagine how monstrous this doctrine must have sounded in the ears of the bishop and his clergy. The Bohemian was seized, and put out of the way at the stake.

Our attention is called to the cases of Reseby and Craw, because the men were foreigners and were martyred. But there were other currents flowing through the country whose course was without observation; and not a few things occurred during the century to show that long before Knox appeared, the views which he preached had begun to be promulgated in Scotland.

4. **The Lollards.**—Who *the Lollards* were, for example, is not quite clear—some tracing them to a German, others to an English (and Wickliffite) source. But in any case this is certain, that a sect bearing that name, and holding many of the distinctive articles of the Protestant faith, did prevail (especially

in the west of Scotland) from the beginning of the fifteenth century, and that their success was great enough to cause the most serious alarm. The Scottish Parliament of 1425-26 directed the bishops to make diligent search after them, and, what is still more suggestive, every graduate in the University of St. Andrews was required to swear that he would do his best to guard the Church against their machinations. If the leaven had not been very formidable, these precautions should have been sufficient to extinguish it. But the efforts at suppression seem to have proved abortive; for toward the very close of the century—in 1494—the aid of the King's Great Council itself was solicited by the Church authorities. The infection had spread, it appeared, to the higher classes. A considerable company of lairds and ladies—chiefly from Kyle and Cunningham—were charged by Bishop Blackadder of Glasgow with holding such 'heresies' as these, that images and relics ought not to be worshipped; that after the consecration of the Mass there remains bread; that every faithful man and woman is a priest; that the Pope is not the successor of Peter; that priests may have wives; that the Pope forgives not sin, but God; that we should not pray to the Virgin Mary; and that we are not bound to believe all that the doctors of the Kirk have written. The preaching of such doctrines must have been intolerable to the hierarchy. And yet—the circumstance is significant—the prosecution came to nothing. Whether the rank of the parties protected them, or whether the King was averse to the use of severe measures, or whether, as is hinted, the wit of one of the defenders turned the whole thing into ridicule, the trial collapsed, and the Lollards (for so they are expressly called) returned to their homes triumphant.

It is important to note such incidents as these, because they help to explain the subsequent course of events. The corruptions and abuses of the Church might in time have provoked an insurrection, and the likelihood of that happening was made the greater by the spread of intelligence. But Popery would not have given place to Protestantism if the people had not come to be acquainted with what the Bible teaches about God and His worship. Through the circulation of the Scriptures, and the distinct blessing which accompanied it, a religious revival took place. Many were led to see not merely the errors of the Church of Rome, but the saving truth that is in Jesus Christ, and through their zeal in diffusing a knowledge of the gospel, the mass of the people were not altogether unprepared to appreciate and welcome the great revolution of the Reformation.

1. *How long did the Church of Rome rule over Scotland?*
2. *What was the first thing which excited the desire for reformation?*
3. *Name some of the most intolerable corruptions.*
4. *What helped to increase the dissatisfaction?*
5. *By whose translation of the Bible was the movement helped?*
6. *Give the names of two early Scottish martyrs.*
7. *Who were the Lollards?*
8. *What were their tenets?*

CHAPTER IV.

THE REFORMATION.

IN the autumn of 1525, public and unmistakable notification was made of the fact that 'the Reformation' had reached the shores of Scotland. An Act of Parliament was then passed, in which it was ordained that 'forasmuch as damnable heresies are being spread in divers countries by the heretic Luther and his disciples, and this realm and lieges have firmly persisted in the holy faith since the same was first received by them, and never as yet admitted any opinions contrary to the Christian faith, but ever have been clean of all such filth and vice: therefore, that no manner of person—stranger—that happens to arrive with the ship within any part of this realm, bring with them any books or works of the said Luther's, his disciples or servants, dispute or rehearse his heresies or opinions unless it be to the confusion thereof, under the pain of escheating of their ship and goods, and putting of their person in prison.'

This Act was published in all the ports and burghs of the realm in July, and only a month later a note had to be issued by the King in Council calling the attention of the Sheriff of Aberdeen to the ascertained fact that the interdict had been broken, and that some of Luther's books were in actual circulation within his jurisdiction. The plague had indeed arrived.

It was in 1517 that Luther nailed his theses to the church door of Wittenberg, and the challenge thus given by him awoke echoes in every university and church circle of Europe. Outside his own country he was generally denounced as a heresiarch, but his pamphlets were eagerly bought and read nevertheless, and much mischief had been done before the priests of the old faith realized what was happening. Luther's books, however, did not constitute the only literature which was smuggled about this time into Scotland. A considerable trade was carried on between our East Coast towns and the Low Counties, and our skippers from Leith and elsewhere found it profitable to bring over as part of their cargoes parcels of Tyndale's Bible, which in those days was printed at Cologne.

A movement like this could not, under any circumstances, have been met as was that of the previous century. The printing press is a more formidable adversary to fight than the copyist's pen, and with a wide and exposed coast, it would not have been possible for the Church to bar the incoming of pestilential publications from the Continent. If, therefore, the same blessing had attended the circulation of Tyndale's Bible as undoubtedly went with Wickliff's, the number of individuals influenced would have been far greater, and the dissatisfied and protesting element dangerously increased. But with all that, the movement would not so soon have attained to national dimensions, or resulted so rapidly in the overthrow of the established ecclesiastical institutions, if it had not been for several things in connection with which we cannot but recognise the marks of Divine interposition.

1. **The Leaders.**—One notably providential circumstance was the raising up of a succession of remarkable men as the leaders of the movement. The success of all movements depends more upon this than upon anything else. Numbers may become a rabble if they have no head; and a very few may become mighty if they have a man of genius to guide them. It is happily no longer a sign of narrowness to think highly of Knox and the Regent Murray. Such writers as Froude and Carlyle agree in asserting that no greater Scotchmen ever lived, and we shall therefore be held to say nothing out of the way when we claim for a cause which enlisted them a *prima facie* importance, and point to their leadership as having contributed providentially to its

triumph. Knox and Murray, however, were not the only outstanding men of that age. Among the laity were not a few who possessed statesman-like gifts, and among the preachers were men who would have been distinguished in any time.

2. **John Knox.**—Of this class three men stand out with the greatest prominence: Patrick Hamilton, the proto-martyr of the Reformation; George Wishart, its first evangelist; and John Knox, the earliest of that grand series of Church statesmen of whom the Church of Scotland has such good reason to be proud. We can make room only for a short outline sketch of the life of the last of the three.

Knox was born in 1505 at Haddington, and was educated at the Grammar School there and at the University of St. Andrews. About 1530 he was ordained to the Roman Catholic priesthood, but he seems to have occupied himself more with academic than with ecclesiastical pursuits. It was while studying the works of Augustine that he began first to doubt about the religion in which he had been brought up, and took to reading the Scriptures in the original; and it was while he was nominally teaching philosophy that he first betrayed to his students the drift of his mind. He did not, however, openly avow himself a Protestant till 1542, when he was taken into the family of Douglas of Longniddry as a tutor to his boys. In this post he remained for several years, devoting a considerable portion of his time to the instruction of the neighbourhood in the truths of the gospel. When Wishart came to Haddington in January 1546, Knox attached himself to his person, and became the bearer of the sword which it had been the custom to carry before the martyr ever since his life was attempted in Dundee. Such an open identification of himself with the cause of Wishart made Knox of course a notorious man. He had good reason to fear that he might be the next victim selected for the sacrifice; and to save himself he shortly after took a step which resulted in momentous consequences. The castle of St. Andrews remained for sixteen months in the hands of the men who had slain Cardinal Beaton, and during that time it was resorted to as an asylum by many who desired toleration for their religion. Knox followed the example of such, and with his pupils was admitted within its gates at the end of the year. Here, by what we may call a stratagem, he was induced to enter on the public exercise of the Christian ministry, and such power accompanied his sermons and disputations during his seven months of residence in the place, that a great number of the inhabitants renounced Popery and made profession of the Protestant faith by partaking together of the Lord's Supper. The circumstance is memorable on this account, that then for the first time the sacrament was dispensed in Scotland in the scriptural way. There was, however, to be a sad ending of all this. A French fleet arrived to invest the castle, and at the end of July 1547 the garrison capitulated. Knox, with others, was carried a prisoner to France, and for twenty long months he laboured at the oar of a French galley.

How he came to be released is unknown, but when he gained his freedom he immediately proceeded to England. There he was received with great cordiality by King Edward VI., and was provided through him with a sphere of usefulness. For five years he laboured in connection with the Church of England, and might have attained to high place in it if he could have persuaded himself that it was in all respects rightly constituted. But he disapproved of its discipline and its episcopal government, and although he accepted the office of King's chaplain, he refused at once a parochial charge and a bishopric. When Bloody Mary ascended the throne his life was once more put in peril, and he fled for security to the Continent. There, in Geneva, he made the acquaintance of Calvin, by whose persuasion he was induced to accept the oversight of an English congregation in Frankfort. But he had little encouragement to remain there, and he left it after a short and troubled ministry. In the autumn of 1555 he paid a visit to Scotland, and contributed greatly, by his counsels and preaching, to rally the drooping cause of the Reformation; but while at home he received a call from Geneva to become the pastor of the English congregation in that city, and he saw it to be his duty to return to Switzerland.

The three years that followed were the quietest and perhaps the happiest of his life. He was greatly esteemed in Geneva, so much so, that when he left it the freedom of the city was conferred upon him. He was in constant communication with Calvin and others of the leading continental divines. And to crown all, he had an attractive domestic circle, wife and mother-in-law and children making for him a peaceful home. But all the while his heart was in Scotland, and in the cause for which he had already done so much; and when, at last, an earnest invitation was given to him by a number of influential men, pressing for his return, he had no difficulty in seeing his way to accept. He sailed from Dieppe on the 22d of April, and landed at Leith on the 2d of May 1559. He was now fifty-four years of age, not very robust in body, but with a latent energy which was at last to be fully called forth, and the entire remainder of his life and strength was given to his country.

It may truly be said, when Knox at this time passed up Leith Walk to Edinburgh, the hour had come and the man. The tide of the Reformation had had its ebbs and flows, but now the critical moment was approaching when it was to be definitely settled, at least for a generation, on which side the nation, as such, was to be. While Knox's eloquence and sagacity—his force of character and fearlessness—would have made him an acceptable recruit at any stage of the conflict, he was specially welcome now, when the final struggle was to take place.

3. **The Crisis.**—The state of things was this: Protestant doctrine had been widely diffused among the people, and the popular faith in the old system had been thoroughly undermined. The Reformation cause also had its competent leaders, who were able to hold their own, both socially and intellectually, against all

comers. But then on the other side there was the Queen Regent, —Mary of Guise,—with all the power of France at her back, and associated with her were many of the nobility and all the priesthood. If the Queen had been wise, she would have continued, as she had been doing for a time, to tolerate and temporize. But she had made up her mind that the movement must by all means be arrested, and the result was a civil war, which had the immediate effect of forcing the Protestants to organize themselves into a distinct party. This party, with the help of England, and under the inspiration of such men as Knox and Lord James Stuart, grew increasingly formidable. One town after another threw off the Papal yoke and established Protestant worship. More and more it became apparent that the cause of Rome was a lost cause; and so it came to pass that the Scottish Parliament, which met in August 1560, was able, with an extraordinary amount of unanimity, to adopt a *Confession* framed on substantially the same lines as that of Westminster; to abolish the Papal jurisdiction; to forbid, under certain penalties, the celebration of the Mass; and to rescind all the laws formerly made in favour of the Roman Catholic religion, and against the Reformation.

4. **Protestantism Established.**—It is rather a memorable circumstance, that this Parliament did not proceed to endow the new Church of the nation. That was an after work. Establishment, or the national recognition of a particular faith, was not at once seen to be the same thing as the direct support of it out of the material resources of the kingdom.

Much, however, had to be done after Parliament had publicly sided with the Reformation. A new ecclesiastical system had to be organized, and for that end a *Book of Discipline* was prepared. This was done at the request of the Privy Council by a committee of ministers; but, of course, the controlling mind of the committee was that of Knox, and the book is usually associated with his name. It is a remarkable composition, and shows how advantageous to the Reformer had been his diversified experiences and education. Row says, Its principles were taken not from the teaching of any other Church, not even from Geneva, but direct from the Scriptures; and we may admit this to be true. But it had not been for nothing that Knox had held intimate intercourse with the greatest English and continental thinkers of his day, and had had so much leisure for reflection afterwards in his quiet retreat at Geneva. Its discipline, technically so called, is severe, so much so, that the council hesitated to put its official *imprimatur* on the book; but altogether it is a wide-minded, catholic-spirited production, such as was hardly to have been expected in the age to which it belongs.

A reformed ministry was to be established in room of the priesthood, and for this there was not, to begin with, an adequate supply of men. A smaller man, who was afraid of being charged with inconsistency, would have hesitated to move in these circumstances. He would probably have been content to wait until the supply had increased. But Knox was too great and too practical an administrator to sacrifice vital interests to technicalities. The country required to be evangelized. That was the problem pressing for solution. And without caring, apparently, whether he was misjudged or not, he recommended the setting up of a temporary order of officials, who had *prima facie* a suspicious resemblance to bishops. These he proposed to call *superintendents*. The land was divided into ten or twelve districts, and over each of these a superintendent was placed to see to the planting of kirks and to the securing of a ministry for them. There are some, of course, who have seen in this arrangement a testimony to Prelacy, but what is most visible in it is clearly the inspiration of common sense. The system is expressly described as a temporary expedient; and that Prelacy was not intended to be set up is plain from this, that one of the first superintendents was the good old baron, Erskine of Dun.

Associated with the superintendents were pastors and doctors, whose special work is indicated by their names, and elders and deacons, with whose functions we are familiar.

Nor did the book concern itself only with ecclesiastical matters, strictly so called. It entered largely into the subject of school and university education, and developed at once that scheme to which Scotland owes so much. 'Of necessity we judge it,' say the compilers, 'that every several kirk have one schoolmaster appointed; such a one, at least, as is able to teach grammar and the Latin tongue.' Then in towns of any consequence 'colleges' or grammar schools are recommended to be instituted for instruction in the higher branches. And finally, increased support is urged to be given to the three then existing Universities of St. Andrews, Glasgow, and Aberdeen.

But all this required money, and for that the patrimony of the Church was naturally looked to. But here, in this connection, broke out one of the 'saddest scandals' of the period. Already some of the landlords had laid hold on ecclesiastical property, and were appropriating it to their own use. 'With the grief of our hearts,' say the authors of the *Book of Discipline*, 'we hear that some gentlemen are now as cruel over their tenants as ever were the Papists, requiring of them the teinds and whatsoever they before paid to the Kirk, so that the papistical tyranny shall only be changed into the tyranny of the lord and laird. . . . Even gentlemen, barons, earls, lords, and others must be content to live upon their just rent, and suffer the Kirk to be restored to her right and liberty, that by her restitution the poor, who heretofore by the cruel Papists have been spoiled and oppressed, may now receive some comfort and relaxation, that their teinds and exactions be clean discharged, and no more taken in times coming. The uppermost cloth, the corpse-present, clerk mail, the pasche offering, tiendale, and all handlings upon a land [exactions in the country], can neither be required nor received of good conscience.'

Knox's theory was to restore at the outset to the oppressed people all that it had been the custom to extort from them by mere superstition, and of the remaining Church property he suggested the disposal in such a way as to provide a modest maintenance for the professors, teachers, and ministers, and to

C

meet the wants of the poor. This was sketched out only as the ultimate destination of the endowments, for to begin with there was of course a heavy charge in the way of meeting vested interests. The priests who refused to conform (there were, however, very many who did so, though they were not always very acceptable accessions to the Protestant ministry) were not allowed to remain in their incumbencies, but none of them that needed were allowed to starve.

These grand schemes, however, were rendered in a considerable measure abortive by the cupidity of the landholders. It is an obvious calumny to say, that what attracted the barons to the Reformation at the first was their hope of sharing in the spoils of the Church, for, with the Court against them, nobody could have expected the revolution which so soon took place. But it casts a shadow on the subsequent sincerity of some of them, that they made their Protestantism pecuniarily so profitable. And yet, let us not refuse to confess that there was, after all, a certain wild justice in their depredations. The ancestors of these men had given land to the monks under the belief that they could transact for them with Heaven; and the monks accepted the gifts as for value promised or bestowed. The vanity of the bargain was now disclosed, and goods were reclaimed that had been taken on false pretences.

5. **The First General Assembly.**—On the 20th of December 1560, the first General Assembly was held in an old chapel in the Cowgate of Edinburgh which had been dedicated to St. Magdalene. It was not an imposing convocation in point of numbers. There were just six ministers in it, and four-and-thirty elders. But its quality was high, both in respect of the ability and of the social position of its members, and its decisions carried greater weight than always followed the larger gatherings convened afterwards. It met by its own authority. Its right to do so was at an early period challenged by Maitland of Lethington. 'The question is,' said he, 'whether the Queen alloweth such conventions.' 'If the

liberty of the Kirk,' it was replied, 'should depend on the Queen's allowance or disallowance, we are afraid we shall be deprived not only of Assemblies, but of the public preaching of the gospel.' 'No such thing,' argued Maitland. 'Well,' said Knox, 'time will try; but I will add, take from us the freedom of Assemblies, and take from us the evangel.' Knox was right. Events proved that, in thus claiming at the outset an inherent autonomy for the Church, a principle was laid down of supreme practical importance. The Reformers had no idea of doing anything in secret, or doing anything of which they required to be ashamed; and they suggested to the Queen that if she entertained any suspicions about them, she might send a representative of the Crown to hear their deliberations. Hence arose the office of Lord High Commissioner. But from the beginning the freedom of the Church was emphatically asserted, and the presence of a Commissioner was never held to imply any right on the part of Majesty to constitute or dissolve General Assemblies.

Under the arrangements made for the occupation of the field, Knox became minister of Edinburgh; and in the Cathedral of St. Giles he continued till his death to deliver from week to week those powerful harangues in which the gospel was faithfully proclaimed, and the principles of the Christian religion fearlessly applied to all the conditions of social and political life.

6. **Character of the Reformers.**—Like all great men who have been instrumental in their day in achieving radical changes, Knox has been exposed to an extraordinary amount of abuse. He has been called a bigot, a brute, and a hypocrite. The destruction of the monasteries has been ascribed to him. He is thought of, in certain circles, as having committed a nameless atrocity in making Queen Mary weep. And those who know nothing of religious earnestness themselves, have been quick to see sinister purposes in everything he did. But as the clouds of prejudice disperse, his character comes out ever more and more clear and grand. It is now made certain that the religious houses fell a prey to popular

outbursts, which Knox, instead of inciting, did his best o control. Mary's tears look greatly less precious in the light of Froude's revelations of her conduct. And as to his sincerity, his whole life and writings speak for him. The more one looks into the history of the period, the more plainly it is seen that the conflict was waged around positions, the very nature of which irreligious politicians cannot understand. The deepest questions in debate were not about Church Government and Forms of Worship. Men were brought face to face with far profounder problems—with problems touching the very heart of the Christian life. It was keenly realized that Christ had been displaced from His position of Mediator, and that no satisfactory reformation could be accomplished unless He was restored. This is seen at once in the defences of the Reformers and the fulminations of their enemies. Both went below the surface of things to the root of the matter, and made it plain what the battle was felt to be about. Knox taught 'that there is no other name by which men can be saved but that of Jesus, and that all reliance on the merits of others is vain and delusive; that the Saviour having by His one sacrifice sanctified and reconciled to God those who should inherit the promised kingdom, all other sacrifices which men pretended to offer for sin are blasphemous, and all men ought to hate sin, which is so odious before God that no sacrifice but the death of His Son could satisfy it.' For this teaching the Papal authorities passed upon him a sentence of death; and as he was then furth of the kingdom, they burnt him in effigy. The truth is, that 'the life' in the Church was then struggling to manifest and extend itself, and that the Roman Church of the time represented the antagonistic elements of anti-Christianism and unbelief. What occurred was not a mere intellectual renaissance, but a spiritual revival.

Hamilton, Wishart, Knox,—these are the outstanding figures which meet the eye as it traces the Reformation movement back from its completion to its rise. But they were by no means the only remarkable men who were raised up to aid in the work.

Not to speak of the first preachers, some of whom seem to have possessed high gifts as such, few ages have produced more accomplished scholars than George Buchanan and John Row, or abler politicians than Maitland of Lethington and the Regent Murray.

7. **Mary Queen of Scots.**—It must be admitted that the course of public events subsequently to 1560 contributed materially to the confirmation of the change which was then made in the religion of the country.

James V. was the last of the Scottish kings before the Reformation. He was a nephew of Henry VIII. of England, and for a time it seemed as if he might follow in his uncle's footsteps. But his own priesthood, and the influence of his wife Mary of Guise, prevented that, and he died leaving behind him unmistakable proofs of his devotion to the Papacy. The crown at his death passed to his daughter, an infant, the unfortunate Mary Queen of Scots, whose whole education from first to last came to be of a kind to fill her with hatred of the Reformation. Just one year after the disestablishment of the Church of Rome—that was in August 1561—Mary landed at Leith from France, and was welcomed by the people with joyful acclamations. She was young and beautiful, and had the reputation of being clever and accomplished, and there was something romantic and captivating in her return as the widow of a French prince to occupy the throne of her ancestors. It did not seem likely that a girl queen received in such a way, would do much, at least soon, to disturb the order of things. But she had not been many days in Holyrood before the Reformers saw that they had good cause for anxiety. She ordered Mass to be celebrated in her private chapel; and she so fascinated the nobles who came to her Court by her charming manners, that the roughest of them refused to listen to a word against anything she did. The reaction came so quickly, and was so influential while it lasted, that, if nothing had occurred to arrest it, the restoration of Popery before many years had passed would almost certainly have been accomplished. But happily for the cause which she sought to overthrow, Mary wanted the personal qualities needed to make her triumph. She was passionate, imprudent, and unprincipled, and in seven years she was not, as she hoped to be, the unchallenged mistress of Scotland, with Protestantism under her feet, but a fugitive in England, looking forward to a scaffold. That the tide which came in with her accession did not sweep all before it, was due in great measure to Knox, who gave fearless expression through the pulpit to what is now uttered through the press—the voice of public opinion. But even his efforts would not have availed, if it had not been, first, for the Queen's foolish love for Darnley (a youth of nineteen); next, for the suspicions roused about foreign conspiracies, and by the favour shown to Rizzio; and, lastly, by the murder of her husband, and her shameless marriage with Bothwell. No popularity could have borne up against such a succession of false steps. The tradition of her beauty and of her charm of manner has procured for the hapless Queen champions in every age, especially among the young and romantic, and among those who are profoundly impressed either by the wickedness or the vulgarity of Protestantism. But candour among historians is no longer an unknown quality, and among people not led away by fancy or prejudice, it is now generally conceded that Mary, morally, is a most forbidding character, and that while her talent, if regulated by prudence, might have ruined the Reformation, her wickedness and folly contributed to its confirmation.

1. *How did the Scotch become acquainted with Luther's teaching?*
2. *Name some of the leaders of the Reformation.*
3. *Where was Knox born? and when?*
4. *When did he avow himself a Protestant?*
5. *What service did he render to Wishart?*
6. *How was he led to become a preacher?*
7. *What position did he fill in England?*
8. *Give some account of his life abroad.*
9. *When did he return to Scotland?*

10. *Describe the condition of things when he arrived.*
11. *Give an outline of his plan for the work of the Church.*
12. *What did he propose for education?*
13. *How were the Church funds disposed of?*
14. *When was the first Assembly held?*
15. *What question was raised about its meeting?*
16. *What influence had Mary Queen of Scots on the Reformation?*

CHAPTER V.

PRESBYTERY AND PRELACY.

AFTER the death of Mary, Scotland never ran any very serious risk of relapsing into Romanism. The Spanish Armada, which sailed in 1588 with the design of restoring the Papal supremacy in England, would of course have brought the cloud back upon us if it had been successful; but it was called 'invincible' only by its organizers. It is not very likely that Spain would have subdued Britain under any circumstances; and at no subsequent time was the cause of the Reformation ever very directly threatened.

1. **Tulchan Bishops.**—But the Church was on that account by no means through the breakers. A new struggle soon began for the right to shape itself according to its own convictions. It might seem at first that it could not signify much to any one but itself what form of government it chose to adopt. In a very short time, however, it was made clear that there were various parties keenly and personally interested in the matter. Among these, to begin with, were some of the nobles, who saw with concern the life interests of the old bishops and abbots gradually lapsing, and the lands they held falling into the possession of the Church. To prevent this catastrophe, as they regarded it, an informal Assembly, called in history '*The Convention of Leith*,' was held in 1572, and there, through the influence of the Regent Morton and others, an Act was passed providing for the restoration of the old hierarchical titles. The men who brought about this change had no idea of making prelates after the old fashion. Their plan was simply to create an order of middle-men, through

whom they might themselves get possession of the ecclesiastical endowments. A simple or obsequious minister, with perhaps a flavour of vanity in him, was to allow himself to be named (say) Bishop of Dunkeld. As such he would have certain rights which he might enforce, but to these, as a condition of his appointment, he was to sign his title away to his patrons. The arrangement was received in the country with derision. The men who consented to play the ignoble part of catspaw to greedy nobles were nicknamed 'Tulchan Bishops,' in allusion to the device of placing a stuffed calf beside a cow to induce her to yield her milk, and the new dignitaries were for a season more laughed at than feared. Especially was this the case when the succeeding General Assembly refused to recognise this sham episcopate, and when it seemed to be settled that Morton's bishops were to have no ecclesiastical standing. But, all the same, the thin end of the wedge was introduced. The idea was started that Episcopacy might ultimately become the form of government in the Scottish as in the English Church. It was assumed that toward the settlement of that point the Court or the State had a right to contribute. And around this centre a battle raged which did not end for a century.

2. **The Course of the Controversy.**—The era during which the question of *Presbytery* versus *Prelacy* came into greatest prominence was that which extended from 1572 to 1638. The other principle, that of the right of the Church to shape its own constitution, was also then necessarily discussed; but it was during the later period, the distinctively 'covenanting' period, that it was brought most conspicuously to the front, along with questions which cut to the quick, bearing on the right of private judgment and on civil and religious liberty.

When Knox died, in 1572, James VI., the son of Mary and Darnley, was but a child, and the kingdom was under a regency. This office the Earl of Morton held from 1572 to 1578. In the latter year the young King—a boy of twelve—was persuaded and helped to take the reins of Government into his own hand. That meant, of course, that others ruled in his name; and, unfortunately, these others were not men qualified to guide him rightly. His was not a fine character at the best, and it was not made better by the society of his first favourites. These were a Scoto-Frenchman whom he created Earl of Lennox, and (strange to say) a brother-in-law of Knox, a younger son of Lord Ochiltree, whom he made Earl of Arran. The state of things brought about by this change soon became intolerable, and there took place in 1582 what is known in history as 'The Raid of Ruthven.' A party of dissatisfied nobles seized the King's person. The favourites were for a time driven from the Court, and under new and better influences the Church and country prospered. But the tide again turned. The Earl of Arran regained his old ascendancy over the King, and James, who believed the Ruthven Raid to be inspired by some of the ministers, showed a disposition to be revenged. Andrew Melville, the champion of Presbytery and the successor of Knox in the leadership of the Church, was obliged to flee, and in 1584 what are known as THE BLACK ACTS of this period were passed. These Acts ordained that no Assembly could meet without the King's permission; that no one was to be at liberty to say a word in public or private against the Government; that to decline the judgment of the Privy Council *in any cause*, was to be regarded as high treason; and that all ministers were to acknowledge the bishops as their ecclesiastical superiors. Such laws produced momentary consternation, and were the cause of some suffering; but that they were the outcome of passion and not of deliberation, was almost absurdly proved by subsequent events. Three years later, in 1587, an Act of what we would call disendowment took place, attaching the temporalities of all benefices to the Crown. This made the maintenance of a dignified Episcopacy well-nigh impossible. But in 1590 the fickle King took a further step. He had married a Danish princess, and on coming home with his bride he had found that, thanks to the Presbyterian ministers, things

had gone well in his absence. This, and his kindly reception on
returning, seems to have put him in high good humour. He
attended the General Assembly, and made a speech which produced quite a furor of enthusiasm. 'He fell forth praising God
that he was born in such a time as the time of the light of the
gospel, and to be king in the sincerest Kirk in the world. The
Kirk of Geneva,' he went on to say with a sneer, 'keepeth Pasche
and Yule [Easter and Christmas]; what have they for them?
They have no institution. As for our neighbour Kirk in England,
it is an ill-said Mass in English, wanting nothing but the liftings
[the elevation of the host]. . . . I charge you, my good people,
ministers, doctors, nobles, gentlemen, and barons, to stand to
your purity; and I, forsooth, so long as I brook my life and
crown, shall maintain the same against all deadly.' No wonder
that after such an oration 'there was nothing heard for a
quarter of an hour but praising God and praying for the King.'
Nor did the fit pass immediately. In June 1592, Parliament
repealed the Black Acts, gave its formal sanction to Presbyterianism, and directed that presentees to parishes should be
settled without regard to the concurrence of any bishops. Thus
the episode of the Ruthven Raid seemed to have, in the long run,
ended happily enough.

3. **Question of Toleration.**—But again the clouds gathered in the
sky. James and the Protestant clergy came into collision on the
subject of extending toleration to some of the Popish nobles.
Theoretically, perhaps, the King was in the right. Religious
liberty was not so well understood in those days as it is now.
But we must not judge of the conduct of the two parties by
abstract standards. The times in which they lived were peculiar.
James was not only King of Scotland, but the heir apparent of
the English throne. His vain and vacillating character was well
known to those who were plotting in France and Spain and elsewhere for the restoration of the Papal supremacy. And the
question of whether reactionaries of a dangerous type should be

welcomed at Holyrood or debarred from it was one of practical politics. There was no daily press to discuss the subject. The preacher, rightly or wrongly, was forced to become the tribune of the people. And out of the controversy thus raised sprang another scheme for licking the Church into a shape in which it would be less inconveniently aggressive.

It was in connection with this agitation that Andrew Melville addressed to the astonished King his famous remonstrance.

'I must tell you,' said he, 'there are two kings and two kingdoms in Scotland; there is King James, the head of this commonwealth; and there is Chris Jesus, the King of the Church, whose subject James the Sixth is, and of whose kingdom he is not a king, nor a lord, nor a head, but a member. We will yield to you your place, and give you all due obedience; but again I say you are not the Head of the Church. You cannot give us that eternal life which we seek for even in this world, and you cannot deprive us of it.'

Such boldness was not likely to be acceptable to one whose views of the Crown prerogatives were always growing higher. He now evidently came to the conclusion that Presbyterianism would never tolerate his freehanded management of affairs, and that Episcopacy on that account behoved to be re-established.

He proceeded to the work of restoration with considerable astuteness. First, he asked the General Assembly to appoint Commissioners with whom he could confer on the business of the Church. The Assembly did not see the trap laid for it, and consented. Then he got Parliament to declare that the clergy constituted the Third Estate of the realm, and he invited the Commissioners to take their seats in the House with the nominal rank of bishops. The Assembly now saw the snare, and interposed its veto. But James contrived to bring together meetings of ministers and elders, whom he succeeded in overawing, and the upshot was that, with the apparent consent of the representatives of the Church, three men were appointed to the Bishoprics of Ross, Aberdeen, and Caithness.

4. **King James in England.**—Three years later, in 1603, Elizabeth died, and James became King of England. The new atmosphere into which he was now introduced seemed to intoxicate him. Speaking at the celebrated Hampton Court Conference, which was held soon after his coronation, he congratulated himself on having reached 'the promised land, where religion was professed in its purity, where he sat among grave, learned, and reverent men, and that now he was not, as formerly, a king without State and honour, nor in a place where order was banished, and beardless boys would brave him to his face.'

Sentiments like these did not bode well for the Kirk of Scotland. Nor was there anything more promising in his proclaiming on the same occasion a maxim which had become a favourite with him, 'No Bishop! no King!' It had, in fact, come to this, that, in his judgment, Presbyterianism was incompatible with monarchy, and that its suppression was a State necessity.

The story of the process by which the King brought about the submission of the Scottish Church illustrates the threat which he uttered at Hampton Court against the Puritans. 'I'll make them conform,' said he, 'or I'll harry them out of the land.' First of all, he set himself to suppress the right of free Assemblies, and after a struggle he succeeded. Of the bold men who ventured to hold a meeting without his permission, six were tried for high treason and banished. Then Andrew Melville was summoned to London and committed to the Tower, where he remained for four years. At the end of that time he was permitted to retire to France, and he died a professor in the Protestant College of Sedan. The next step was to secure to the bishops precedence in all Church Courts, or, as it was expressed, to get them made constant Moderators. This was done in a packed and corrupted Assembly, held in 1610. Previously to that, Parliament had obsequiously repealed so much of the Act of Annexation (1587) as applied to the secularization of the bishops' lands. And suitable means having thus been provided, Prelacy full fledged was imposed upon the land, three men going to England to receive consecration from a Church in which, as was supposed, the apostolic succession was surer, and coming back to communicate the grace they had got, independently of all presbyterial action.

It is curious that the people seem to have borne all this with patience. They may have been angry, but they were certainly not violent. It was different, however, when the King, on the occasion of his first visit to his native country, in 1617, proposed to introduce visible changes into their forms and habits of worship. An Assembly, called and inspired by himself, passed five new regulations, which, from the place in which they were proposed, are known by the name of the Five Articles of Perth. These ordained—(1) That the Lord's Supper should be received kneeling; (2) That it might be administered in private; (3) That baptism also might be private; (4) That children should be confirmed; and (5) That Christmas, Easter, etc., should be observed as holidays. Some of these points are not now considered very material; and it is consequently assumed in certain circles that the outcry that was raised against them was ridiculous. But it need scarcely be said that a deeper explanation must be sought for the agitation aroused, than what is supplied by the subject-matter of the precepts read in the light of the nineteenth century. The King had claimed the right to regulate the worship of the Church. His appeal to the Assembly, such as it was, was merely *pro forma*. There was good cause to apprehend that there was a plot on foot to assimilate the Scottish Church in all respects to what was regarded as the half reformed Church of England. And the changes proposed brought the contemplated revolution home to those most interested.

No open insurrection occurred, however, till a number of years afterwards. At first the new ordinance was a dead letter. Ministers and people kept to the old fashions, and the bishops were afraid to provoke an *émeute* by interfering. But as things went on the prelates grew in dignity and boldness, and less and less toleration was shown toward those who refused to conform. A crash sooner or later was inevitable, and it came in a very dramatic way.

5. **Charles I. and Laud.**—James died in 1625, and was succeeded by his son Charles I., a much more respectable man in many ways, but with faults of character quite as conspicuous. Charles believed devoutly that he reigned by a divine right, and that he was entitled to demand from his people submission to his will in all things; and when opposition was offered to him, he had no hesitation in making and breaking engagements with the leaders of it, on the principle apparently that no faith was to be kept with rebels. He paid his first visit to Scotland in 1633, and gave the people there a taste of what he had in store for them, by keeping the Sabbath after the manner of the Book of Sports, and by forcing the Parliament to confer upon him power to regulate ecclesiastical vestments. What he did in these matters was, no doubt, by the advice of Laud, afterwards Archbishop of Canterbury, who accompanied him on this occasion, and who seems to have been much affected by the baldness of our Scottish ritual. Hitherto Knox's Liturgy, as it is called, had been in use where needed. It had been prepared to meet the necessities of post-Reformation times, when ministers were few, and public worship could not have been maintained in many places at all, except by the agency of 'Readers' using the Book of Common Order. As vacancies were filled up by educated men, the Liturgy naturally fell aside. But, of course, it regained its position under the Episcopal system, and this was the form which Laud met when he went with the King to St. Giles'. That a high Anglican such as he was should have been dissatisfied, is not to be wondered at. He went home with the determination to provide for the benighted Scotch a better Service Book; and sure enough, what was meant to be a great boon to our nation in due time arrived. It arrived, not in the

booksellers' shops, to be bought by anybody who wanted it. It arrived, not for delivery to the General Assembly, to be examined and approved. It arrived with a sovereign law behind it, ordering every minister to provide himself at once with two copies on pain of deprivation, and directing its immediate adoption by all the congregations of the Church.

We talk sometimes now-a-days as if our fathers made much ado about nothing. How often, for example, has fun been made of the incident which marked the introduction of Laud's Service Book into St. Giles'? The Dean of Edinburgh, clad in his surplice, had just begun to read it, when Jenny Geddes, an apple-woman from the neighbourhood, flung her stool at his head, crying, 'Fause loon, dost thou say Mass at my lug!' With what lofty pity have English and Scottish Episcopalians smiled at this outbreak of ignorant fanaticism! 'What was the good dean doing?' they say,—'Only reading a prayer! Think of the perverted condition of a people who could not stand so much as that!' But who that knows anything of the subject, does not know that 'reading a prayer' had no connection with the outburst? The Scottish people had no objection to the reading of prayers when it was necessary. The indignation was caused, first, by the character of the Service Book itself (it was merely an amended edition of the Roman Missal); and, secondly, by the manner of its introduction. No doubt, we of the nineteenth century are a law-abiding, much enduring people. The Scotch have borne patiently at times what would have provoked a rebellion in Ireland. But we venture to affirm that an imposition anything like that which Charles I. attempted in 1637, could not be made in 1882 without evoking a burst of indignation as threatening to the Crown as the riot whose dramatic beginning we have just described.

When an avalanche is about to fall, the shout of a single hunter is sufficient to set the mass in motion. The nation was ripe for insurrection against the intolerable rule of Charles and his advisers, and the protest of Jenny Geddes became the signal for a general uprising. So far as Scotland was concerned, the revolution was accomplished with perfect quietness, and without a drop of bloodshed. The Privy Council in Edinburgh at once recognised the situation, and permitted the formation of what was virtually a provisional government. Four Committees—or *Tables*, as they were called—were established—one for the nobility, one for the barons, a third for the towns, and a fourth for the Church; and under the direction of this body the negotiations with the King were carried on, and likewise the proceedings which followed.

6. **The National Covenant.**—First, however, a step was taken which contributed more than anything else could have done to the success of the movement. This was the renewing of the *National Covenant*. The Covenant had been drawn up in 1580, and had been then signed by the King and many of his subjects. It was a bond engaging its subscribers to adhere to and defend the doctrine and discipline of the Reformed Church of Scotland. It was now wisely thought that by catching up the spirit of the past in this way, the religious enthusiasm of the nation would be awakened, and the personal devotion of all who were in sympathy with it secured. And the result showed that there was no mistake in this calculation. On the 1st March 1638, in the Greyfriars' Church, Edinburgh, after an address by the Earl of Loudon, and prayer by Alexander Henderson, the signing of the Covenant began. All ranks and all classes signed it—nobles, gentry, ministers, the mass of the people. The immense sheet of parchment which had been prepared was soon filled, and late comers had to seek corners where to place their initials. Very many were in tears, and yet there was gladness in the sorrow, indicating a happy consciousness that the nightmare under which they had been groaning was over, and that the dawn of a better day had begun.

'To this much vilified bond,' it has been said, 'every true Scotsman ought to look back with as much reverence as Englishmen do to their Magna Charta. It was what saved the country from absolute despotism ; and to it we may trace back the origin of all the efforts made by the inhabitants of Britain in defence of their freedom during the succeeding reign of the Stuarts.'

7. **The Glasgow Assembly.**—What happened in the interval, between March and November, when the famous Glasgow Assembly was held, need not be particularly rehearsed. The history of that period shows the King acting with the characteristic infatuation and duplicity of his family, and the people open to guilelessness to be moved by any act of kindness but resolute to obstinacy in the rejection of whatever tended to the restoration of the old order of things. 'I intend not to yield to the demands of these traitors the Covenanters,' wrote Charles himself. 'And as concerning the explanation of their damnable Covenant, I will only say that so long as this Covenant is in force, whether it be with or without explanation, I have no more power of Scotland than a Duke of Venice would have. I will rather die than suffer it.' This was a declaration of war *a outrance;* and when the General Assembly, which he had been persuaded to call in the hope of composing things, met on the 21st of November, he had very plain indication given him that the patience of his Scottish subjects had also reached its limit, and that they meant to maintain the liberties of the Church at all hazards.

The Assembly of 1638 was socially one of the most influential that ever sat in Scotland. It was composed of 140 ministers and 98 ruling elders—the latter including 17 noblemen of the highest rank, nine knights, and 25 landed proprietors. Alexander Henderson, minister of Leuchars, was chosen Moderator, and the Marquis of Hamilton was present as Lord High Commissioner. It began serenely in the interchange of courtesies between the Moderator and the Commissioner—Henderson being profuse in his professions of loyalty to the King in all civil matters. But the wind at once changed when serious business was proceeded with. It immediately appeared that this Assembly, in its representative character, claimed a sovereign right to carry out the convictions of the Church as to its own position and duty. In the exercise of that right it abolished the Episcopal form of Church government, and removed the bishops from their offices—declaring at the same time as of no effect the Five Articles of Perth, and the Ordinances about the Service Book. The Marquis of Hamilton did not stay to countenance these bold acts of defiance of his master's will. He left protesting at an early stage. But his absence, though deeply lamented, was not considered to affect the essential authority of the Assembly. The Moderator, by a happy allusion to the zeal of the Commissioner for King Charles' honour, suggested an argument which was felt to tell powerfully on the other side. 'All who are present,' said he, 'know the reasons of the meeting of this Assembly; and albeit we have acknowledged the power of Christian kings for convening of Assemblies, yet that may not derogate from Christ's right, for He hath given divine warrants to convocate Assemblies, whether magistrates consent or not. Therefore, seeing we perceive his grace my Lord High Commissioner to be so zealous of *his* royal master's commands, have we not also good reason to be zealous toward *our* Lord, and to maintain the liberties and privileges of His kingdom?' The Assembly sat from the 21st November to the 20th December, and was dismissed by the Moderator in an eloquent closing address, which ended with these words: 'We have now cast down the walls of Jericho; let him that rebuildeth them beware of the curse of Hiel the Bethelite.'

8. **Reasons for the Uprising of the People.**—Men will judge of this remarkable convocation from their several standpoints. An Erastian will pronounce it lawless—Episcopalians will call it fanatical—and that numerous class of persons who have no faith in pure motives in any connection will account for it by saying that the lairds were angry because of the resumption of the bishops' lands. But no man of intelligence with any candour will

hesitate to acknowledge that there were things about the Assembly of 1638 which none of these theories explain. In the first place, it was obviously the outcome not of sectional, but of national dissatisfaction. Then the speeches delivered in it were on the whole singularly moderate and well-toned. And further, the men composing it were many of them so distinguished for their piety, learning, and weight of character, that it is extremely difficult to conceive of them as carried away by a mere blind and unreasoning madness.

Anyhow, there must have been good cause why a whole people should have thus risen as one man against the Prelacy to which they had been accustomed for thirty years, and under which many of them had been born. It had become hateful to them, not so much as a Church system, but as a political system. It represented the idea of foreign interference with their internal affairs—an impertinent attempt on the part of strangers to rule them in the domain of conscience. They had borne the burden long, as a patient and peaceable people is so ready to do, and because no suitable means of deliverance appeared. But they had been groaning for years under the load of oppression, and when at last the opportunity for relieving themselves of it presented itself, they seized it with an eagerness and a unanimity which spoke volumes for their previously pent-up indignation.

Besides, apart from all abstract questions as to Church government, and as to the ways in which new forms may warrantably be introduced, the Scottish people had had abundant opportunities for comparing Presbyterianism and Episcopacy together, and for coming to a conclusion as to the suitableness of each to the genius and condition of an intelligent and independent nation.

'The earnestness,' says Dr. Rainy in his reply to Stanley, 'with which Presbyterianism was maintained, was due to something else besides the confidence men had in their theoretical conclusions about Church government. Everything that is theoretically good and true has a practical value in itself, from which it receives daily confirmation. So it was with Presbyterianism. Presbyterianism meant organized life, regulated distribution of forces, graduated recognition of gifts, freedom to discuss, authority to control, agency to administer. Presbyterianism meant a system by which the convictions and conscience of the Church could constantly be applied by appropriate organs to her affairs. Presbyterianism meant a system by which quickening influence, anywhere experienced in the Church, could be turned into effective force, and transmitted to fortify the whole society. Presbyterianism meant a system in which every man— first of all the common man—had his recognised place, his defined position, his ascertained and guarded privileges, his responsibilities inculcated and enforced,—felt himself a part of the great unity, with a right to care for its welfare and to guard its integrity. From the broad basis of the believing people, the sap rose through sessions, presbyteries, synods, to the Assembly, and thence descending diffused knowledge, influence, organic unity through the whole system. . . . Our fathers felt instinctively that the changes thrust upon them threatened to suppress great elements of good—not mere forms alone, but the life which these forms nourished and expressed. When Episcopacy shall have trained the common people to care, as those of Scotland have cared, for the public interests of Christ's Church, and to connect that care with their own religious life as a part and a fruit of it, then it may afford to smile at the zealous self-defence of Scottish Presbyterianism.'

9. **The Church Leaders of the Time.**—In the outline given above, we have sought to supply a bird's-eye view of the history of the Church from the outside, a sketch of how it was shaped and directed by external influences. But we shall get a very imperfect idea of the real condition of affairs during the period reviewed, if we do not go within the gates and look at things from the interior.

And here, first of all, it seems desirable that we should make the acquaintance of some of the men by whose personal influence the time was fashioned. It is certain that some fancy pictures exist in this connection. A common notion is that the Presbyterian ministers of that period were a set of ignorant, obstinate persons, who thwarted the King through pure perversity. Alas! the truth is that they were, as a whole, only too easy and pliable. If it had not been for a few stronger-minded men who stood by the helm in all weathers, the ship would often have been allowed to drift. It is, however, just as great a mistake to suppose (as with our characteristic nineteenth century self-complacency we are so apt to do) that the clergy as a rule were uncouth and unlettered, and that even the leaders were, in respect of piety and learning, a long way behind their critics in the present age.

10. **Andrew Melville.**—The name of Andrew Melville has been mentioned once or twice. Who was he? He was a younger son of a Laird of Baldowy, who, with most of the gentlemen of Angus, was slain 'in the vanguard of the field of Pinkie.' After learning all that the Montrose schools could teach him, he went to St. Andrews, which he by and by left 'with the commendation of the best philosopher, poet, and Grecian of any young master in the land.' Next he proceeded to Paris, where he studied for two years, and where he became so expert in Greek that he could declaim in it fluently. From Paris he went on to Poitiers, and afterwards to Geneva, where, through the recommendation of Beza, he was appointed Professor of Latin— an office which he held for five years. During this time his chief study was theology, in which he had Beza for his master; but he had lessons also in the Oriental tongues from Cornelius Bonaventura. When Melville got back to his native land again, in 1574, he found that his reputation had preceded him. The Regent Morton invited him to become his domestic chaplain, but the aspirations of the young scholar inclined toward a professorship, and he accepted instead the appointment of Principal of the University of Glasgow. The list of what he taught in that capa-

city almost takes one's breath away. It included Greek, Hebrew, Mathematics, Moral Philosophy, Natural History, Theology, and the Exegesis of the Old and New Testaments. 'His learning and painfulness,' says his nephew in his Autobiography, 'was mickle admired, so that the name of the college within two years was noble throughout all the land, and in other countries also. Such as had passed their course in St. Andrews came in numbers there, and entered scholars again under order and discipline, so that the college was so frequented that the rooms were nocht able to receive them.' With all his learning, Melville anything but realized the novelist's ideal of a sour and narrow Puritan. One of his favourite pastimes was writing Latin verses, and his pleasantry was so irrepressible that he was followed by a ripple of kindly laughter even to the Tower. But he had strong convictions, and he was perfectly fearless in maintaining these. Like many other scholars of the highest rank, he saw no trace in the Greek New Testament of any office like that of a 'Lord Bishop.' He was not long in his own country without seeing many evidences of the mischief which was being done by the attempt to force Prelacy on the Scottish people. And he threw all the weight of his influence and accomplishments into the Presbyterian scale. To him especially we are indebted for the *Second Book of Discipline*, in which the constitution of the Church is defined with extraordinary ability and precision. No better justification could be offered for the aversion which was then felt to King James' Episcopacy than what was furnished by the fact that its establishment rendered necessary the banishment of such a man. He was the greatest Scotchman of his day. His departure from Geneva was deplored as an almost irreparable loss. The Universities of Glasgow and St. Andrews offered him in succession the highest places at their disposal. And when, after four years of imprisonment, he was allowed to go into exile, he was welcomed at once to a continental professorship. One's blood boils even now to think that it was in the power of an unprincipled pedant like James to deprive his country of the services of a scholar like

Melville. And in any case this will be allowed, that the circumstances just described as attendant on the introduction of Prelacy, were not of a kind to prepossess us in its favour.

11. **Robert Boyd.**—Another man whose character and learning give a very different impression from that which prevails, in certain circles, of the age in which he lived, was Robert Boyd of Trochrigg. 'All accounts,' says Dr. Walker in his *Cunningham Lectures*, 'represent him as a most accomplished scholar. A friend said of him, with perhaps some exaggeration, that he was more eloquent in French than in his native tongue ; and Livingstone tells us that he spoke Latin with perfect fluency, but that he had heard him say, if he had his choice he would rather express himself in Greek than in any other language. The Church of Boyd's adoption [that of France], which had given Andrew Melville a chair in one university and Sharp a chair in another, was not slow to do honour to their brilliant countryman. He was made a professor in the University of Saumur ; and there for some years he taught theology. He was persuaded, however, in 1614, to come home and accept the Principalship of the Glasgow University.' 'Boyd's great work,' adds Dr. Walker, 'is his *Commentary on the Epistle to the Ephesians*. A work it is of stupendous size and stupendous learning. There is more in it than in the four quarto tomes of Turretin. Its *apparatus criticus* is something enormous. The Greek and Latin Fathers, the writers of the Dark Ages, the Protestant and Romish theologians of his own time, Justin and Irenæus, Tertullian and Cyprian, Clement and Origen, Augustine and Jerome, Gregory Nyssen and Gregory Nazianzen, Anselm and Bonaventura and Bernardo, Calvin and Rollock, Bellarmine and Pighius, are all at hand to render and to receive replies.' Boyd's character was as noble as his learning was great. 'He was,' says Livingstone, 'of an austere-like carriage, but of a most tender heart. Notwithstanding of his rare abilities, he had no account of himself, but a high account of every other man's

parts, when he perceived any spark of grace and ingenuity [ingenuousness] ; but where these were not, no man was such a severe censurer.' 'He died in his prime, under fifty years of age.' One would expect to hear of a man like that, that he was held in increasing honour in his country ; but here, too, appeared the mischievous influence of the policy of the time. 'Though he was far from extreme in his Presbyterianism, he was found to be less tractable than the King and his advisers expected, and was obliged to resign his office. But [happily] he was long enough in Glasgow to leave the impress of himself on some of the young men destined to distinction in the Church in after years.'

12. **David Calderwood.**—One other name may be referred to—that of David Calderwood. He was not a member of the 1638 Assembly, but his value was so thoroughly well known that, according to Baillie, he was invited to occupy a chamber near that of the moderator in order that he might be always near at hand for consultation — a high compliment, seeing that the Assembly contained an extraordinary number of the ablest men of all ranks then living in the country. 'Banished,' says Dr. Walker, 'for nonconformity, Calderwood found a home in the Low Countries, where he wrote his great work, the *Altare Damascenum*. It is the most serious attack on Diocesan or rather Anglican Episcopacy which I suppose has ever been made in this country. Patiently and perseveringly Calderwood goes over the whole system, tearing it to pieces as it were bit by bit. The Bible, the Fathers, the Canonists are equally at his command. It does our Church no credit that the *Altare* has never been translated. It seems to have been more in request out of Scotland than in it. The large and beautiful edition I possess was printed in Amsterdam so late as 1700. Among the Dutch divines he was ever "ementissimus Calderwood."'

13. **The Age Unappreciated.**—These are only a sample of what

the age furnished. 'The first century of Presbyterianism in Scotland,' says Dr. Walker, 'was one of incessant struggle. During that period you can hardly say that it got twenty years of quiet and peaceful ascendancy. And yet the Scottish Church produced several divines recognised as of the first class among continental Protestants; it founded an exegetical school from which came commentaries upon all the books of the New Testament and a considerable number of the books of the Old; and when, after a long down-trampling, it reclaimed and regained its rights in 1638, it was able to send representatives to the Westminster Assembly who could hold their own in every respect, and perhaps more than their own, in one of the most venerable and learned Church conventions of Christian history.'

How it is to be accounted for it would not be easy to say; but there can be little doubt that in the English mind, and in the minds also of a certain class of Scotch people, the impression prevails that those who of old resisted the imposition of Prelacy on this country were men of the type of Sir Walter Scott's Habakkuk Mucklewrath. It would be well if the truth were better known. The leading Presbyterian ministers of that time were not in the least like the half-educated English Dissenting village preachers of a past generation, nor were they at all like the ridiculous fanatics whom our own great novelist has created. They were many of them the sons of gentlemen, who had received the best education which the age afforded, and whose learning would have enabled them to make very short work indeed of the great majority of their critics in the present day. It may or may not be foolish to prefer Presbyterianism or Episcopacy; it may or may not be a pity that our fathers refused to conform in religious matters to the example of England. But one thing is certain, that those who then acted for us were not men of whom we have any cause to be ashamed, and that for what they did they were able to render fairly weighty reasons.

14. **Spiritual Life.**—There is yet another point of view from which the Church of that period should be looked at, in order that a just idea may be formed of its character. We have evidence of the most interesting kind that it was spiritually prosperous. In many parts of the country there was a very scanty supply of the means of grace, and there ignorance and religious indifference prevailed. But other localities were more highly favoured, and, in some of these, revivals took place of which memorials remained for several generations. One such awakening occurred, for example, at Stewarton, in connection with the preaching of Mr. David Dickson of Irvine. Dickson was one of the most accomplished men of the time. From Irvine he was transferred to theological professorships, first in Glasgow, and then in Edinburgh. He devoted himself to Biblical studies, and conceived, and so far carried out, the plan of having a Scotch commentary on the whole of Scripture. 'His plan,' says Dr. Walker, 'was to assign particular books to men competent for the work, and to him we owe it that we have Ferguson on the Epistles, Hutchison on the Minor Prophets, Job, and the Gospel of John; Durham on the Song of Solomon and the Book of Revelation. Dickson put his own hand to the work. He published English Notes on Matthew and the Epistle to the Hebrews. His exposition of the Psalms is not unknown to Christian readers still, and, besides, we have from him annotations in Latin on the whole of the Epistles.' Such was the man under whom there originated a great religious movement which continued for five years,—from 1625 to 1630, —and which produced a marked change throughout the whole Ayrshire valley which is traversed by Stewarton water.

But a more remarkable event still was the extraordinary awakening which resulted at the Kirk of Shotts from the preaching of John Livingstone. This was in 1630, on the Monday after a communion. Livingstone was then only twenty-seven, and he had no settled charge, but his gifts were known, and he was pressed to preach, sorely against his own inclination.

'When I was alone in the fields,' he himself writes, 'about eight or nine in the morning, before we were to go to sermon, there came such a misgiving of spirit upon me, considering my unworthiness and weakness, and the multitude and expectation of the people, that I was consulting with myself to have stolen away somewhere and declined that day's preaching; but that I thought I durst not so far distrust God, and so went to sermon and got good assistance.' To this sermon, under the blessing of God, not fewer than five hundred persons ascribed their conversion.

15. **John Livingstone.**—To every Cavalier every Roundhead was a hypocrite. In the eyes of an Anglican, Puritanism is superstition or worse! And we need not be surprised to hear that by some writers John Livingstone is referred to as a Covenanting fanatic. When one thinks of that communion Monday at Shotts, one cannot help wishing that we had more such fanatics. But there are quarters in which the resistless power of his preaching will win for him less respect than such facts as the following, mentioned by Dr. Walker :—' Livingstone was a scholar such as we shall not readily fall in with in these days in the Church. He knew Hebrew, and Chaldee, and something of Syriac. He had tried his hand, he says, at Arabic. He was sufficiently acquainted with French and Italian to be able to make use of French and Italian books. He could read the Bible, too, in Spanish. And now in his exile [he was one of the Scotchmen whom the rulers thought not fit to live in their own land, and who had been driven in consequence to seek shelter in Holland] he desired to do something whereby the knowledge of the only true God might be more plentifully had out of the original. So he set himself first of all to revising the best Latin text of the Old Testament Scriptures, comparing it with the original Hebrew, intending to print the Hebrew and Latin side by side in separate columns. This work was actually done, and was ready for the press, when the friend died who had consented to bear the responsibility of giving it to the world.

What became of the fruit of Livingstone's scholarship I do not know; but,' adds Dr. Walker, 'the fact of it may help to dispel some misconceptions, and give truer notions of Presbyterian learning in the seventeenth century.'

The quotation leads us back to think again of the scholarly attainments possessed by many of the Scottish ministers of that time; but the learning of the two eminent revival preachers we have named was not their most marked distinction. They were men of extraordinary piety and fervour, and what is chiefly remembered about them at this day in Scotland is the notable blessing which attended their efforts to persuade men to believe the gospel. It is a most imperfect idea which the ordinary historian gives of the age, when he dwells on the battles about Church government as if these made its greatest incidents. A glance beneath the dust raised by these battles reveals a busier life, occupied with the exposition of Holy Scripture and with the bringing of individual souls under the power of a world to come.

1. *Who were the Tulchan Bishops?*
2. *In what respect was the liberty of the Church at this time interfered with?*
3. *Describe the Raid of Ruthven, and its effects.*
4. *Give the date and substance of the Black Acts.*
5. *When and under what circumstances did James speak well of Presbytery?*
6. *What great lesson did Andrew Melville teach the King?*
7. *Indicate the effect on James of his accession to the throne of England.*
8. *How did the King succeed in Episcopizing the Church of Scotland?*
9. *Describe the character of Charles I.*
10. *How did he reveal his character during his first visit to Scotland?*
11. *What was the real cause of the rising of the people against Laud's Service Book?*
12. *What was the National Covenant?*
13. *When was the Glasgow Assembly held?*
14. *Describe its composition and work.*
15. *How do you explain the uprising of the people?*
16. *Give some account of the Church leaders of the time.*
17. *What erroneous impressions in this connection are abroad?*
18. *What was the spiritual condition of the period?*
19. *What do we know about John Livingstone?*

CHAPTER VI.

UNDER THE COMMONWEALTH.

'THE opening of the General Assembly of 1638,' says Hill Burton, 'may fairly vie with that of the Long Parliament as a momentous historical event. It was the earlier in time. Had it not been, perhaps the Long Parliament also might not have been. At that juncture, so far as England alone was concerned, the looker-on would have said that the Court would prevail, and that without a struggle. The organization for the collection of ship-money got the prerogative out of its only remaining difficulty, the supply of money capable of supporting a standing army. All things had the aspect of a monarchy serene and absolute, such as Englishmen knew only from specimens on the other side of the Channel. This General Assembly takes precedence in history as the first meeting of a body existing by constitutional sanction, yet giving defiance to the Court. It assembled under royal authority, the King being, through his Commissioner, an element of its constitution.'

Not many months after this famous Assembly, the Scots were required to take up arms in defence of their liberties. Charles refused to recognise their right to adopt whatever form of Church government they chose, and he marched an army to the border to enforce submission to his authority. But he discovered that the subjugation of the Presbyterian 'Tables' would be by no means an easy task. A well-appointed Scottish host under the command of General David Leslie gathered around Dunse Law to repel the invader, and the King, considering discretion in the circumstances to be the better part of valour, consented to a compromise. This was in August 1639. He was by no means satisfied, however, and in the following year he purposed to resume the offensive. The Parliament he summoned refused to grant him the needful supplies, and he hastily dissolved it; but Convocation continued sitting after the dissolution, and agreed to help him. With its assistance a fresh force was organized and marched northwards. But the Scottish leaders had now learnt wisdom from the abortive conflict of the previous summer. They did not wait to be attacked. Knowing something of the King's weakness, and of the distracted state of affairs in England, they crossed the Tweed, and met the force moving to assail them in the neighbourhood of Newcastle. The battle which took place there was not a bloody one. The English were out-generaled, and, although their rout was complete, they lost only some forty or fifty men. Nevertheless the incident turned out to be one of high historical importance. What occurred that day had a material influence on the destinies of the empire. 'The battle,' says Hill Burton, 'by which the Scots forced the passage of the Tyne was so momentous that, in critical interest, it may well rival the famous passage of the Rubicon.'

1. **Opening of the Long Parliament.**—One consequence of it was the calling of the Long Parliament, that extraordinary assembly which continued to sit for so many years, and under which took place some of the most memorable events in English history. Newcastle was taken by the Scottish army. York was threatened. The King had not resources enough at command to carry on the contest. And now, as formerly, he resorted to negotiation. Before a suitable treaty, however, could be arranged, it was necessary to have the concurrence and help of the Legislature. For this and other reasons the country was asked again to send representatives to St. Stephen's, and the appeal issued in the election of a House of Commons which contained an unusual number of able men, but which very speedily showed itself to be a formidable embodiment of the national indignation and dis-

content. The battle of Newbury was fought in September 1640. Negotiations with a view to peace commenced in London on the 26th of October following. And the Long Parliament began to sit on the 3d of November thereafter. There was, however, much to be done besides attending to the affairs of Scotland. One of the first acts of the new Parliament was to arrest and bring to trial the chief instruments of the King's tyranny, Strafford and Archbishop Laud. Another was to release from prison a number of individuals who by their directions were suffering for conscience' sake. And it was not till August 1641 that the Scottish Commissioners were able to turn their faces homeward with a new and favourable treaty in their pockets. But their long residence in London was not without advantage to their country. Three of them were ministers—Henderson, Blair, and Baillie—who all preached frequently, crowds attending them just as they did Irving and Chalmers in later days. These men became intimately acquainted with the Puritan leaders, and thus in many respects paved the way for the intercourse which took place in the years that followed.

2. Oliver Cromwell.—These years were stirring ones in the history of England. Charles and his Parliament came to an open rupture, issuing in civil war, and the conflict brought to the front *Oliver Cromwell*, who first achieved a great reputation as a military leader, and afterwards became virtual sovereign of the country under the title of Lord Protector of the Commonwealth.

In the early stages of this struggle, the Scots were in hearty sympathy with the English Parliament. *The Solemn League and Covenant*, although first drawn up by Henderson, was (in 1643) first adopted by an Assembly in which the English and Scottish nations were alike represented; and that famous Westminster Assembly of Divines, to which we owe our Confession of Faith and the Larger and Shorter Catechisms, was not, as many imagine, a convocation of Scottish Presbyterians, but a council of English Episcopalians, Presbyterians, and

Independents called together by the Long Parliament, and in which certain Scottish Commissioners sat by special invitation to give advice and assistance, but not to vote. As long as this Assembly was sitting—from 1643 to 1649—the relations of England and Scotland were most intimate and friendly. In the beginning of the latter year, however, signs of a breach appeared. Charles, with whom all along the quarrel had been, was no longer alive to trouble them, and the pressing question came to be, Who should be his successor? To Cromwell that question presented no difficulty. He was in principle a Republican, and his idea was that the Government should go on as before with the administration in the hands of the people. But the Scots had no dislike to monarchy. They had a special interest in the Stuart family as having sprung from among themselves. They had also some reason to think personally well of the legitimate heir to the throne. And so they no sooner heard of the execution of the King, than they proclaimed his son, Charles II., his successor. The act brought them into collision with the now powerful head of the English Commonwealth, who in 1650 marched an army of his Ironsides across the Tweed, defeated the army gathered to oppose him at Dunbar, and ultimately subjugated the whole country. Until the death of Cromwell, in September 1658, Scotland lay helpless at the feet of a master who exercised virtually despotic powers alike in civil and ecclesiastical matters. But the despot was intelligent and benevolent. He dissolved the General Assembly as summarily as he had dismissed the Rump of the Long Parliament, and the two parties in the Church, the Resolutioners and Protesters, were peremptorily restrained from tearing each other to pieces. But there was no Prelacy heard of in his day. Lay patronage was everywhere abolished, and no earnest minister was suffered to be molested while he was engaged in any spiritual work. The Lord Protector was an Independent in his Church principles, and as such was very unacceptable to the Presbyterians. He was a conqueror also, who was ruling the Scots against their

E

will. But the time of the Commonwealth in Scotland was at once materially and religiously a time of unusual prosperity ; and now that the soreness which it caused is completely healed, we may allow ourselves to think of it with, on the whole, grateful satisfaction.

3. **Abolition of Episcopacy.**—We have glanced but lightly over this period,—from 1638 to 1658—from the Glasgow Assembly to the death of Cromwell,—but these twenty years mark an extraordinary era in the history of our island. The Imperialism of the Court provoked a violent reaction alike in Church and State, and Prelacy and Monarchy came for a season to be in equal disrepute. The Scottish Presbyterian leaders must have felt like men that dreamed when, in place of requiring to maintain a defensive attitude against England, they were invited by the rulers of that country to join with them in maturing plans for establishing one evangelical Church to which both nations might adhere. Events in those days proceeded with startling rapidity. In 1637, Episcopacy was the recognised form of Church government in Scotland, and the only question debated was as to whether the sovereign will of Archbishop Laud in regard to a new service book was to be obeyed or not. Six years later, not only was Episcopacy displaced in Scotland, but a Bill had passed the English House of Lords ordaining that after the 5th November 1643 there should be no archbishops, bishops, etc., in that country ; that all their titles should cease, determine, and become utterly void ; and that their possessions should return to the King. The Westminster Assembly was convoked to fill in a right way the void that had thus been caused ; and it is a remarkable circumstance, that as the Scotch Commissioners, though present only as assessors, contributed materially to the framing of the documents prepared, so their country has been impressed most deeply and enduringly by its proceedings. Few Englishmen know that the Jerusalem Chamber was the place in which the Standards of the Presbyterian Churches were

elaborated; or realize that the Shorter Catechism framed there is to this day the religious text-book of our schools, and the Confession of Faith the test of the orthodoxy of our ministers.

4. **What gave Scotland its Influence.**—It was owing in part to the peculiarities of the political situation that Scotland was allowed and enabled to take the influential part it did in the direction of affairs in these days. But the power it exercised was due also to its being represented by men of remarkable ability. Argyle, Loudon, Johnston of Warriston, among the laity, were well able to hold their own even with the astutest members of the Long Parliament; and in no age has the Church had leaders of greater learning, piety, and power than Henderson, Rutherford, and Gillespie.

5. **Samuel Rutherford.**—Regarding Rutherford, Dr. Walker writes: 'It is not easy to find any one in Church history to compare with this remarkable man (though I have sometimes thought of Bernard of Clairvaux),—a man of power, I may say of genius,—fresh, bold, penetrating, to whom no subject came amiss, teeming with intellectual energy, distinguished for his learning, but never cumbered by it; the greatest scholastic of our Presbyterian Church, and yet, we are told, the plain and faithful teacher,—the fiercest of Church leaders, and the most devout of saints,—equally at home among the tomes of Aquinas, and writing letters to a poor congregation.' 'Rutherford's letters,' Dr. Walker adds, 'are so far as I know the only letters, two centuries old, which are still a practical reality in the religious life of Scotland, England, and America.'

6. **George Gillespie.**—'The name (we again quote Dr. Walker) you most naturally conjoin with Rutherford's is that of his younger contemporary, George Gillespie. He was but a stripling when he entered the field of authorship, in his work on the English Popish ceremonies. You do not wonder at the im-

pression made. With an entire self-composure, the youthful theologian debates the points at issue with the great writers opposed to him. The whole literature of the subject seems to be at his call. I do not suppose that from the pen of so young a man there has ever appeared in our country a work of more consummate learning.'

7. **Alexander Henderson.**—Henderson was more of a statesman than a theologian—at least, he was too much involved in active work to find time for literary composition. But the estimation in which he was held by his contemporaries was extraordinary. Baillie, in describing to a friend consultations held before the Assembly of 1638, writes that there was but one opinion about his fitness for the Moderatorship—the only question was as to whether he could be spared from the floor of the house. 'We were somewhat in suspense,' he says, 'about Mr. Henderson,—he was incomparably the ablest man of us all for all things,—but we expected then much dispute with the bishops and Aberdeen doctors, and we thought our loss great and hazardous to tyne [lose] our chief champion by making him a judge of the parties.' He was appointed notwithstanding, and earned for himself in the office golden opinions. In the Westminster Assembly his counsels were equally weighty; and when he was at last taken away, he was lamented as one who had rendered to the Church of Scotland services which were second in importance only to those of Knox. He died in 1648. Rutherford lived till 1661, —long enough to see the Restoration, to join with Blair in a vain endeavour to keep Sharp out of the University of St. Andrews, and to hear of his great book, the *Lex Rex*, being burnt by the common hangman. If his summons to a higher court had not come then, his ending would not have been so peaceful as it was. He was one of those whose continuance in existence was reckoned intolerable by the flatterers of Charles, and while he was dying he was called to Edinburgh to answer to an accusation of high treason. The citation happily came

too late. Before he could respond to it, he was 'where few kings and great folk come.'

8. **State of Religion.** — It has been said that the time of the Commonwealth was a time of spiritual prosperity in Scotland. On this point the testimony of Kirkton is most explicit. He admits that the dissensions of the two parties in the Church— the Resolutioners and the Protesters (the former representing the Broad School of the day, the latter the section that was more rigid)—did no little harm ; 'yet,' he says, 'were all these losses inconsiderable in regard of the great success the word preached had in sanctifying the people of the nation; and I verily believe there were more souls converted to Christ in that short period of time than in any season since the Reformation. Nor was there ever greater purity and plenty of the means of grace. Ministers were painful ; people were diligent. So, truly, religion was at that time in very good case, and the Lord present in Scotland, though in a cloud.'

1. *To what in importance has the Glasgow Assembly been likened?*
2. *When did the Long Parliament begin to sit?*
3. *What interest has England in the Solemn League and Covenant, and in our Confession and Catechisms?*
4. *Mention some of the great events which occurred about this time.*
5. *Name some of the Scotchmen who took a prominent part in the public affairs of the period.*
6. *What was the state of religion under the Commonwealth?*

CHAPTER VII.

THE PERSECUTING TIMES.

OLIVER CROMWELL was succeeded in the Protectorate by his son Richard—a man of very inferior ability, and one quite incapable of carrying on the Government which his father had established. A change of some kind, therefore, was speedily seen to be inevitable; and the old question began to pass from lip to lip: 'Why speak ye not a word of bringing the King back again?' The interest felt by the Scots in Charles II. was, of course, natural enough. He was of their own kith and kin. But they had had some experience of him when he came across from Holland, after his father's death, to measure swords with Cromwell. He had then manifested a perfect readiness to sign any number of Covenants, and had been crowned at Scone as a Presbyterian; but he had convinced all the discerning men who came into contact with him that he was utterly destitute of seriousness and sincerity. And they might have hesitated now, in the remembrance of that, to rush thoughtlessly into his arms. But the infatuation of the time was upon them. There came a reaction from Puritanism, just as, twenty years before, there had been a reaction from Imperialism. The King was asked to come and take his own again; and in no part of the kingdom was his return hailed with more enthusiasm than in the most ancient portion of his dominion.

1. **The Restoration and its Immediate Consequences.**—The Restoration took place in 1660; and within a year the Scots learned that if Cromwell had chastised them with rods, it was the

purpose of his successor to chastise them with scorpions. The King was settled without conditions. It is true that an effort was made, both before he left Breda and after his return to London, to move him to consider favourably the wishes of his Scottish subjects in regard to ecclesiastical matters; but these negotiations were committed to the conduct of Mr. James Sharp, who looked mainly after his own interest; and apart from that, it is humiliating to read of the attitude which our country-folk assumed in their intercourse with the ruler whom they had called back from his exile. Instead of maintaining an independent position, and boldly naming terms to him, they waited meekly and almost timidly to learn what good it was going to please him to grant to them.

Nor had they long to wait. 'In the latter end of March,' writes Mr. W. Row in his *Life of Blair*, 'the Parliament did rescind all the Acts approving the National Covenant, the Solemn League and Covenant, and the abolishing of bishops in Scotland; and they rescinded all Acts for Presbyterian government, yea, all Parliaments since 1637, as wanting lawful authority — only tolerating Presbyterian government during the King's pleasure.'

A wet sponge was thus applied to a most remarkable episode in British history. The Glasgow and Westminster Assemblies, Cromwell and the Long Parliament, the Confession of Faith, the Solemn League and Covenant, were all blotted out at one sweep from the page of history. Scotland was to be dealt with as if for twenty years it had been dreaming, and the thread of its history was taken up at the point where the dream began. Of course, the King very soon spoke out more explicitly about the government of the Church. The Presbyterian system, which was to be tolerated during his pleasure, was summarily set aside on the 6th of September, when the obsequious Scottish Council ordained the Lyon King-at-Arms 'to pass to the Market Cross, and make publication of his Majesty's pleasure for restoring the Kirk to the right government of bishops, and to require all his subjects to compose themselves to a cheerful acquiescence and obedience to the same . . . commanding all, if they find any failing in their obedience thereto, or doing anything to the contrary, that they commit them to prison till the Council give further orders.' 'This,' says Row, 'was looked upon as the saddest proclamation that had been in Scotland these twenty-five years bypast, overturning all that had been done these years, by the setting up of archbishops, bishops, etc.; and that not, as his grandfather, by Church judicatories, though corrupted, and by several steps and degrees, but *per saltum*, and that by his sole power and authority, by virtue of his supremacy, or rather because it was his pleasure so to do.'

2. **A New Episcopate.**—Of the old set of bishops only one remained, and it was necessary to reorganize the order. This was done by sending four men to London to receive consecration from the English Episcopate; and when the new prelates entered Edinburgh wearing the blushing honours which had been conferred upon them in Westminster Abbey, the Scottish Parliament passed Acts restoring to them all their ancient prerogatives, temporal and spiritual, reimposing patronage and Episcopal ordination, and requiring all persons occupying places of trust to take an oath abjuring the Covenants.

3. **Archbishop Sharp.**—The leader in this new raid upon Presbyterianism was James Sharp. He was, to begin with, minister of Crail; and as he showed himself to be a man of affairs, he was selected by his Church to represent it at the Court of Charles II. during the formative period of the Restoration. Professor Flint condescends to be the apologist of this man, and maintains that his character was much less black than his contemporaries believed it to be. 'Sharp's decision,' he says,[1] 'to abandon Presbyterianism was only made after Presbytery had been disestablished by the Scottish Parliament.' He only left the ship when it was certainly sinking. He was not a man

[1] *St. Giles' Lectures*, 1st series, p. 203.

to be morally admired, but he was not a moral monster. And so on. It is one of the amiable characteristics of the present age, this attempt to hold the balances perfectly even, and to show that there were good points in the worst of men. But we question greatly whether it can serve any wholesome end to attempt to palliate the conduct of Archbishop Sharp. Nobody believes that Judas joined the company of Christ's disciples with the deliberate purpose to betray Him; and nobody thinks of Sharp as a traitor from the outset. But no twisting of history can hide the fact that he was employed by Presbyterians for the preservation of Presbyterianism—that he saw how things were drifting, and did his best to prevent the Church from taking all possible means to arrest the current,—and that in the end he was base enough to accept a reward for accomplishing what he had been commissioned to oppose. In no other connection could a man act so dishonourably and have honourable men speaking for him. And in the present instance it specially grates upon one to hear a Presbyterian minister apologizing for Sharp when his after conduct to his countrymen and brethren is remembered. No one will excuse his assassination. It was a blunder as well as a crime. But the circumstance of its occurrence has a significance which no criticism will ever overpower. The popular instinct is not in the least likely to have been mistaken. Such aversion as Sharp awakened was not produced by a merely morally weak man who had the misfortune to be misunderstood.

4. **Archbishop Leighton.**—Another of the new bishops was Leighton, a very different man. He was the son of a Dr. Alexander Leighton whom the Long Parliament found in prison suffering from the tender mercies of Archbishop Laud. When the record of these sufferings was read,—he had had his ears cut off, and was hardly able to crawl,—sobs of grief and indignation were heard all over the hall. But the younger Leighton bore no malice against a system which, in certain hands, had

proved so cruel. To him it seemed that questions about Church government were matters of minor moment. He had attained to a strong faith in the central verities of the Christian religion, and in the hope that his countrymen might be induced to think of these only and let other things drift, he lent himself to the execution of a scheme which, in his mind, was to be a moderate Episcopacy, but was so tolerant as that practically nobody was to be disturbed. As might have been expected, he soon discovered that he had been cherishing the dream of a Utopia. The imperiousness of his own colleagues on the one hand, and the obstinacy of the Presbyterians on the other, rendered the realization of his conception absolutely impossible, and in the end he retired to the south of England and closed his days peacefully as a parish rector.

5. **The Old Presbyters.**—In the meantime a further step was taken to bring about uniformity. The proclamation of the Council pointed only to what was to be done in the future. But here was a problem handed down from the past: What was to be the position of the ministers already in possession of the benefices? To meet this case, it was decreed, 'That all kirks planted since 1649 should be declared vacant, unless [their present occupiers] be presented by the patrons, and get collation from the prelates before the 20th of September.' 'The pretext was,' says Row, 'because the Parliament of 1649 abolished patronages, putting the power in the hands of the people and Presbytery; and so they judged these ministers, admitted by Presbyteries but not presented by patrons, to have been illegally entered.' The 20th of September came and went, and no such signs appeared of obedience to the Act as seemed to hold out the prospect that the Church would be thoroughly Episcopized. Hence the Commissioner, with a quorum of the Secret Council, took it upon him to issue a new and more imperative edict on the 1st of October. The edict ran thus: 'Whereas there was an Act of Parliament

ordaining ministers entered since 1649 to obtain presentations to their benefices from their patrons and collations from their respective bishops betwixt the date of the said Act and the 20th of September, otherwise their kirks to be declared vacant, etc. Yet, notwithstanding, many ministers ordained since 1649 continue, since the 20th of September, to exercise the duties of their callings, they having neglected to get presentations from their patrons and collations from their bishops,—all which ministers are discharged any longer to exercise any part of their ministerial callings, and all hearers and others discharged to acknowledge them as their ministers, and all heritors and others discharged to pay them any part of this year's stipend ; and they and their families are commanded to remove out of their parishes and presbyteries betwixt the date hereof and the 1st of November.'

It was felt, after this harsh measure was published, that it was too hasty in its requirements, and the time of grace was extended to February 1663 ; but there was no relaxation in its demands, and the result was that nearly 400 ministers were ejected from their charges, and cast for their support on the freewill offerings of their people. This might not have been an unmitigated evil if the ejected clergy and their sympathizers had been let alone. But the idea of tolerating a nonconforming body outside the Establishment was not entertained for a moment. There now began an internecine struggle between the Government for supremacy and the people for liberty ; and the conflict ended only with the overthrow of the Stuart Dynasty.

6. **The Instruments of Persecution.**—Had it been possible to compel conformity among such a people as the Scots at this time were, the means used for that end must have been successful. The Government of the Restoration gave from the first unmistakable proofs of its being possessed of a cruel and unscrupulous energy. It had given warnings to the nobles and clergy alike by striking at Argyle and Guthrie,

and bringing them both to the block; and it had shown itself
to be not afraid of discontent, by keeping on the even tenor
of its way in spite of the secession of two thousand ministers
in one day in England. What made it pursue its tyrannical
course with such confidence for so long a time, was perhaps
the circumstance that it was able to secure such suitable
agents. During the earlier years of the persecuting times the
machinery of repression was directed by men who were believed
by the people to be under some demoniacal influence. Three of
them were renegades—Sharp, Rothes, and Lauderdale. To one—
Sharp—sufficient reference has already been made. Another, the
Earl of Lauderdale, sat as Lord Maitland in the Jerusalem
Chamber as one of the Scotch Commissioners to the Westminster Assembly. He came into Middleton's place as Secretary
of State for Scotland, and till 1680 superintended the various
measures which were taken to force upon the people the blessing
of Episcopacy. These men found willing and worthy tools.
First, there was Sir James Turner, who won his spurs in the
Thirty Years' War. 'How terrible a curse he must have been to
the people,' says Hill Burton, 'can be better understood from
the dry detail of an official report than from all the vehement
and eloquent denunciations that have been heaped upon him by
the sufferers and their sympathizers.' The time came when Sir
James ceased to be on the sunny side of the hedge. His conduct
became the subject of investigation by the Privy Council, and
among the charges brought against him were these :—1. Exacting quartering money for more soldiers than were actually
present ; 2. Fining such as lived orderly ; 3. Fining for whole
years preceding his coming into the country ; 4. Fining one that
lay a year bedfast ; 5. Taking away cattle, etc. But Sir James
was a courteous knight compared with General Thomas Dalziel.
'*He*,' says Hill Burton, 'had served abroad, and of all the foreign
adventurers who had brought evil ways from foreign institutions
and practices, he had brought home the largest stock of ferocity
and rapacity. Others had chiefly served in the centre of Europe,

and in the Thirty Years' War. They had learned enough of evil there; but Dalziel had been doing the work of the barbarous Muscovite far off at the back of Europe.' Bitterly, however, as Turner and Dalziel came to be hated, the feelings they excited were moderate as compared with those which were subsequently called forth by James Graham of Claverhouse. A halo of romance has been thrown around him. He has been represented by the novelist as essentially a gallant soldier, with but a dash of the dare-devil in him. But the instincts of a whole people are not to be disregarded. He had not the excuse to plead of a Muscovite training. He was a Scotchman born and bred, and the record of his cold-blooded cruelties sends a shudder through us even yet.

Think of a defenceless people given up to be ridden over rough-shod by such men as Turner, Dalziel, and Claverhouse, while others like Sharp, and Rothes, and Lauderdale, and Mackenzie directed their operations. We may wonder that they did not succeed in the end in compelling conformity, but we cannot very much wonder that the Scottish nation has never since been very much in love with Prelacy.

7. **Persecuting Methods.**—It is too long a story to tell in detail here, but the general course and character of the events of the period can be easily described. The problem to be solved was how to compel all to accept the State religion, and the methods followed were such as the following :—

Here was a parish of which the minister was a man in the prime of life. He had been ordained in 1650, on the unanimous call of the people, and ever since he had laboured among them so zealously and faithfully as to be universally respected and beloved. But the decree of the Council came directing him on pain of ejection to secure the consent of his bishop and his patron to his continuance in office, and he felt himself shut up to one course. He had studied in St. Andrews, under Rutherford and Baillie, and had drunk in their teaching about the spirituality of the Church and the scripturalness of Presbytery, and he could not conscientiously retain his living on the conditions named. In the winter of 1662–63, therefore, he left his manse and set out with his young family to seek a place where he might rest till the blast was over. No sooner was he gone than his place was filled by one of those young men from the north whom Burnet describes as the worst preachers he ever heard, as ignorant to a reproach, and as being many of them openly vicious. Under these circumstances the parish church was of course deserted. The whole people, from the laird downward, either stayed at home, trying to edify one another, or travelled to a neighbouring church, the incumbent of which was an Evangelical, and whose settlement had taken place before the critical year of 1649. But this state of things was not tolerated long. The curate complained to the authorities in Edinburgh that his ministrations were not being taken advantage of, and a troop of dragoons was sent to the spot to enforce conformity. This was done in a vigorous way. When the Sabbath came round the military commandant appeared at the church door with a list of the parishioners in his hand. The absentees were then noted and duly called upon the same evening or next day to give an account of themselves. If any were without excuse, fines were imposed, and soldiers quartered upon the offenders till these were paid. In this way cruel wrongs were often inflicted. Families who refused to submit were ruined, and the number came to be steadily increased of people without a home wandering in a state of destitution over the country. The poor people bore all this, however, and sharper measures required to be tried. A species of Inquisition, called the High Commission Court, was established for the express purpose of suppressing all dissent. It was made penal for any of the outed ministers to preach anywhere,— even in a barn; and imprisonment, torture, and banishment were resorted to when milder means proved ineffectual.

8. **Battle of the Pentlands.**—That all this could not go on in-

definitely without provoking an *emeute*, was to have been anticipated. The first outburst took place in 1666, when four countrymen interfered to prevent some soldiers from cruelly ill-treating an old man who had fallen into their hands. The two parties came to blows. The fire so kindled spread, and the result was a rising which at one time appeared threatening enough to alarm the capital. In the end, however, it proved to be merely a flash in the pan. The army which the Covenanters mustered was found to be neither sufficiently numerous nor sufficiently well armed to stand against the well-trained forces of the Government. A serious defeat was sustained by it, on the 28th November, at Rullion Green, on the Pentlands. And the rebellion, as it was called, was made the excuse for the exercise of greater severity than ever. The prisoners taken on the occasion were treated shamefully, and the thumbscrew and boot, the favourite instruments of torture used by the Scottish Inquisition, were freely employed to force suspected persons to reveal what they knew or did not know about the rising. Among those who suffered legal murder at this time, was Hugh M'Kail, whose speech on the scaffold in the Grassmarket sent a thrill through those who heard it which, we may say, has continued to be felt by others to this hour.

9. **Reign of Terror.**—So far, however, the severities served their end. A reign of terror was established which for a time produced a delightful amount of conformity. 'All the people,' says Burnet, 'were struck with such terror that they came regularly to church, and the clergy were so delighted with it that they used to speak of that time as the poets do of the golden age.'

One can imagine the shame and indignation with which this spiritual despotism was submitted to. Certain measures of relief came in 1667, when an Act of Indemnity was passed for the Pentland rising. But no religious toleration was granted; and things got back very much into their old condition again, when, in June 1668, the life of Sharp was attempted in the streets of

Edinburgh. The bullet missed its mark, but the archbishop took his revenge on the would-be assassin, who was not found at the time, by worrying anew the party to which he was assumed to belong. It by and by came to be clearly seen, however, that if an end was to be put to the disorder which still continued, the natural leaders of the people—the ministers —would need to be dealt with; and as the story developes, one can see that the political movements of the time were more and more directed to their suppression. The first device resorted to in that connection was a very cunning one. An Act of Indulgence was passed allowing certain of their number to return on specified conditions to their parishes. The conditions did not look very hard, and some were tempted to comply with them. But the majority reckoned the offer a snare, and the effect of the arrangement was to drive a wedge into the mass, which for years after produced heartburnings and divisions.

10. **The Blinks.**—Those who refused the Indulgence were not silenced. In the face of all warnings many of them continued to preach,—sometimes in private houses, sometimes in the fields, —and in spite of fines and imprisonments people would go to hear them. To meet this state of things conventicles were formally proscribed, and laws were passed making attendance on them treason, and officiating at them a capital offence. Nevertheless, field preaching became commoner than ever, and between 1669 and 1679 the extraordinary spectacle was presented of a large portion of the nation meeting Sabbath after Sabbath for worship in open defiance of the law. Because of this very strain upon their feelings, their attention to religion grew to be intense. When men listened to a minister who was risking his life to preach to them, and when they saw on the rising grounds around, sentinels watching for the approach of enemies before whom they themselves might fall, they could not but give unusual heed to the word spoken. The result was that deep impressions were often made, and that that decade was ever

afterwards remembered as a time of blessing and revival. It was the season of *The Blinks*, as they were called. Between the severities which followed the rising of the Pentlands and 'the killing times' which succeeded the assassination of Sharp, there came bursts of sunshine; and although the sky was every now and again obscured by clouds, some of them dark enough, the suffering Church received gracious visitations of the Spirit, which at once compensated it for its actual trials, and prepared it for the furnace through which it was to be called to pass. Many strange tales are told of this time. We read of the communion being observed in the fields. We hear of troopers coming to kill, being arrested by the word, and remaining to pray. We are told of conventicles meeting under the very eye of the enemy. In short, such a state of things existed as we can account for only by supposing that it was then as it had been with the Apostolic Church, when fear came upon every soul, and unbelievers were unconsciously restrained from mischief by the mighty hand of God.

11. **Murder of Sharp.**—But 'The Blinks,' which had been becoming fewer and fainter, finally disappeared in May 1679, when Archbishop Sharp was met on Magus Muir, and deliberately murdered. The incident filled the innocent breasts of the authorities with unutterable moral indignation. They had themselves caused the death of hundreds of innocent persons, and the cruelties they had inflicted on multitudes more had been simply frightful; but then they had 'the law' on their side. 'The law,' to be sure, was of their own making, and it was an outrage on justice. Still it was 'the law,' and they acted according to its forms. Sharp, on the other hand, was stricken down by a band of men who held no legal warrant from them,—and the crime they committed filled them with a nameless horror. We can look calmly at all the acts of that time now,—and no one seeks to justify the tragedy of Magus Muir. But we have come thoroughly to understand that there are such things as 'legal

F

murders;' and there are few Scotchmen who are not prepared to affirm that the crime of Hackston of Rathillet (if he really was the guilty man) was infinitely less horrible than that which his judges committed when they ordered him to be dealt with in the manner following :—

'His right hand was first struck off, and a little after, his left, which he endured with great constancy and firmness. He was next drawn up to the top of the gallows by a pulley, and was suffered to fall down a very considerable way upon the lower scaffold three times with his whole weight. Then he was fixed at the top of the gallows, and the executioner, with a large knife, cutting open his breast, pulled out his heart before he was dead; for it moved when it fell on the scaffold. He then stuck his knife in it, showed it on all sides to the people, saying, *Here is the heart of a traitor.* At last he threw it in a fire prepared for the purpose, and, having quartered his body, his head was fixed on the Netherbow, one of his quarters, with his hands, at St. Andrews, another at Glasgow, a third at Leith, and a fourth at Burntisland.'

A party of enthusiasts, led away by a momentary impulse, may kill a tyrant and not be ruffians. But is it conceivable that the barbarities we have described could have been committed in cold blood by men in the position of judges, if they had not been worse in heart than the murderers whom they condemned?

Anyhow, the assassination was certainly a blunder. The persecution broke out in a fiercer form than ever; and very many lives were, directly and indirectly, lost in consequence. A new test came into use in connection with it. Men and women were asked if they thought the slaying of Sharp was '*murder.*' If they said *No*, or hesitated, they were immediately proceeded against; and punishments of the severest kind were inflicted on people for their *thoughts*.

These oppressions, again, evoked a dangerous spirit in the country. Field meetings continued to be held, and those who attended them came armed. New views also began to be taken of the nature of civil government. Hitherto all the people had stood loyally by the King—denying, indeed, his right to direct them in religious matters, but acknowledging his claim to their submission in all civil concerns. The wearing oppressions, however, to which they had been subjected, led some of them to doubt whether he could be the ruler to whom God meant them to give submission; and they came to the conclusion that, as he was persecuting the Church of God and wasting it, he should be disowned. A bitterer spirit than before thus came to be infused into the struggle, and out of the misunderstandings thereby engendered much trouble arose. It needed now but a spark to set the country in a blaze, and the spark was kindled on June 1, 1679, at Drumclog. An attempt made there by Claverhouse to break up an armed conventicle led to his own defeat; and his defeat brought on the unfortunate battle of Bothwell Bridge.

12. **Bothwell Bridge.**—In that engagement the Covenanting cause was miserably mismanaged; but we forget the unwisdom of its leaders in the atrocities with which the conquerors disgraced their victory. An immense number of prisoners was taken, and of these *twelve hundred* were huddled into Greyfriars Churchyard, where, with no covering but that of the canopy of heaven, they were kept for five long months. At the end of that time those who survived were dispersed in various directions—two hundred and fifty of them being sent away to spend the remainder of their lives as slaves in the West Indies. Happily, perhaps, for the larger number of these, they never reached their destination. The vessel in which they sailed was wrecked on the Orkney coast, and all save a few perished. Of this wretched remainder, two or three lived to come home again at the Revolution; and one wonders what they thought. The crime for which they had suffered so dreadfully was that of striking a blow for liberty to worship God according to their consciences. Did they come to believe that they had been punished righteously, or were

they still of opinion, after all that had come and gone, that those were no criminals who fought at Bothwell and Drumclog?

13. **The Killing Times.**—But the effects of the rising were not felt only by those who took part in it. The 'Killing Times' now came in earnest. Not men only, but women also, and even children, became the victims of a persecution which was at once savage and relentless. The story of John Brown of Priesthill, shot down by Claverhouse like a dog, has fascinated the readers of the history. But there are other incidents quite as horrible. And as we think of them, the wonder grows that the excuse sought was not actually furnished—to give up all Scotland to military rapine. The Duke of York is said to have given it as his opinion that there never would be peace till all the country south of the Forth was turned into a hunting field; and if the Scottish people had not been restrained by considerations of religion, it is more than likely that they would have really provoked a war of extermination.

14. **The Society Men.**—The Covenanting spirit was now most visibly represented by the Society Men — by men who had adopted the principle that the King was no longer entitled to their allegiance. These men—Cargill, Cameron, Renwick, etc.—lived like outlaws, as in fact they were; preaching as they could find opportunity, and keeping alive in different localities the spark of independence. Upon many others the terror of the times fell, and they were quiet and silent for very fear. But nothing could daunt the spirit of those later witnesses, to whom we are certainly indebted for keeping the flag flying when otherwise it would have gone down.

15. **Accession of James VII.**—Charles II. died in February 1685, and was succeeded by his brother James, a Roman Catholic. The new King was no better at heart than his pre-

decessor, and at first the change brought no relief to the Presbyterians of Scotland. But in course of time he found it convenient to issue edicts for the toleration of Nonconformists. He himself was a dissenter from the Established religion, and his proceedings were viewed with the greatest jealousy and suspicion. To meet his own case, therefore, he conceded all over the kingdom liberty of worship, within certain restrictions, and most of the sufferers in Scotland took advantage of the indulgence. The Cameronians, indeed,—as the Society Men were called,—refused to accept a boon which they regarded as incomplete, and as coming from a polluted source. But the majority were glad of rest on any condition, and thus a measure of peace came even before the Revolution.

16. **The Burden of the Guilt.**—It would be unreasonable to charge the persecutions of this period upon Prelacy as a system. If Charles had been a Papist or a Mohammedan, and had held the principles he did, his imperialism would have found an out-gate through other channels. What is conspicuous in this era is the intolerance of *Erastianism*—the assertion of the right of rulers to hold the Church in subjection, and to force conformity to the religion which *they* profess. At the same time, we cannot forget that the representatives of the Prelacy of the period lent their power and influence to support the tyranny of the Government; and, in the absence of any very general expression of sorrow for the part played by the bishops, we may well be excused for not thinking to this day very kindly of Scottish Episcopacy. It is not the pleasantest reminiscence which we have of Leighton, that his father's son condescended to be the colleague of Sharp. In matters of Church government, indeed, he was himself a latitudinarian. He preferred a moderate Episcopacy, but he could tolerate Presbyterianism without a pang. And that very fact renders his concurrence in the attempt to force new forms upon the Scottish people peculiarly gratuitous. The son of a Puritan martyr, therefore, might have had, to say

the least of it, a greater respect for the proprieties than to throw the shield of his name over a scheme of oppression. And in the same line we add, that there is something radically amiss with those who can allow themselves to talk with admiration of the chivalry of Claverhouse, while they see nothing but a sour and half-insane fanaticism in the faith and independence of Renwick or Cargill.

1. *Who succeeded Oliver Cromwell?*
2. *Did the Scots acquiesce in the English arrangements?*
3. *Give the date of the Restoration.*
4. *What great mistake did the Scots make in bringing the King back?*
5. *How did Charles deal with the Scottish Church?*
6. *In what respect was his conduct unprecedentedly bad?*
7. *How was the new Episcopate set up?*
8. *Describe the men selected for bishops.*
9. *What was asked of the Presbyters ordained after 1649?*
10. *How many refused to assent?*
11. *What was the consequence?*
12. *Name the chief agents in the persecution, and describe their character.*
13. *What methods were followed to compel uniformity?*
14. *When and where did the first rising take place?*
15. *What was the consequence of it?*
16. *How did the indulgences tell?*
17. *What were 'The Blinks'?*
18. *Tell the story of Sharp's murder, and the results.*
19. *Give the dates of the battles of Drumclog and Bothwell Bridge.*
20. *What became of the prisoners?*
21. *What new doctrine about kings did the persecutions give rise to?*
22. *On whom lies the guilt of the Killing Times?*

CHAPTER VIII.

THE REVOLUTION ESTABLISHMENT.

ALTHOUGH King James for his own ends assumed, to begin with, a tolerant attitude, it was soon seen that he was politically as pure an absolutist as his brother had been ; and he was a very much more dangerous man, in this respect, that he was a religious fanatic, and was prepared even to risk his crown in the endeavour to reconnect England with the Papacy. As his plans became developed, it grew more and more evident that he proposed to play the different provinces of his kingdom against one another. A Scotch army was to be used to keep down discontent in England. Scotland was threatened with an invasion of caterans from Ireland. And so many insidious steps were taken toward breaking down the Protestant interest, and repressing constitutional freedom, that patriotic men in all parts of the country took serious alarm, and entered upon a course which, if it had not ended in success, would have been treated as treasonable, and brought some of them to the block.

1. **The Prince of Orange.**—James' eldest daughter Mary had married William Prince of Orange, a man of great ability, and a conspicuous professor of the Reformed Faith. Until the alleged birth of an English prince in 1687, Mary was the heir presumptive to the throne. And it was natural enough that she and her husband should have been consulted when there seemed a danger of the inheritance to which they were looking forward being lost through the recklessness of its immediate possessor. With the appearance of a male heir, this title to be regarded as

parties became less manifest; but it was suspected that there was imposition connected with the birth, and in any case the crisis was too serious to admit of excessive attention being paid to the claims of a sentimental legitimacy. Negotiations, therefore, went on as before between Holland and the revolutionary party in England, and at last the hour for striking appeared to have come. The Prince of Orange crossed the Channel with an army, and landed at Torbay on the 5th November 1688. For a month afterwards it continued doubtful whether there would be civil war—King James remaining during that time in London, engaged in consultations as to how the revolution was to be met. Proofs, however, accumulated upon him that his crown was lost, and he resolved to seek safety in flight.

2. **Fall of the Dynasty.**—' On the 10th of December,' writes Bishop Burnet, who had himself come over with William from the Hague, 'about three in the morning, he went away in disguise with Sir Edward Hales, whose servant he seemed to be. They passed the river, and flung the Great Seal into it, which was some months after found by a fisherman near Vauxhall. The King went down to a miserable fisher-boat that Hales had provided for carrying them over to France. Thus a great King, who had a good army and a strong fleet, did choose rather to abandon all than either expose himself to any danger with that part of the army that was still firm to him, or to stay and see the issue of a Parliament. Some put this mean and unaccountable resolution on a want of courage. Others thought it was the effect of an ill conscience, and of some black thing under which he could not now support himself.'

Whatever was the explanation, thus ignominiously fell the Stuart Dynasty, never to rise again. And if the hill-folk in Scotland had been moved by a vengeful spirit, they might have felt a grim satisfaction in picturing to themselves this last of a persecuting race seeking safety for himself in a foreign country, and hiding his kingly person under the disguise of a servant.

William established his authority in Scotland without a great deal of difficulty. A section of the nobles opposed him; the bishops and Episcopal clergy were in general on the Jacobite side; and the Highlanders under Claverhouse (now Viscount Dundee) made a wild attempt to conserve the old order of things. But an iron hand was now put forth which steadily and firmly put down all opposition; and what really perplexed the new King most, was how to compose the ecclesiastical disorders which had been produced by the misrule of the previous six-and-twenty years.

3. **The Scotch Bishops.**—If we may believe Bishop Wordsworth of St. Andrews, it was more by accident than anything else that the Presbyterian Establishment was restored. If the bishops of that day had only shown a little more worldly wisdom, they would, it seems, have got for their Church all that they could reasonably have desired. Here is the story of how the tide came to be lost:—Dr. Alexander Rose, Bishop of Edinburgh, went up to London to have an interview with the new Sovereign, and William received him with the greatest kindness. On separating, the latter expressed '*a hope that the Scotch bishops would be kind to him, and follow the example of England.*' A great opportunity was thus opened up to the Scotch Commissioner. If he had only had the sense and presence of mind to drink of 'the cup of goodwill and mutual support,' which was now 'unreservedly presented' to his lips by the Prince of Orange, the consequence might have been that the Episcopal Establishment would have been left undisturbed. But Dr. Rose unfortunately made a reply which, though it sounds as if it did him infinite credit, was, in Dr. Wordsworth's opinion, in the last degree injudicious.

'Sir,' said the Bishop of Edinburgh, 'I will serve you as far as law, reason, and conscience shall allow me.' Such an answer reads like one which John Knox or Andrew Melville might have given; and if we had met it in their histories, we should probably have admired it greatly. But the very recollection of it is highly provocative to the Bishop of St. Andrews. 'At this,' says he, 'the Prince *not unnaturally* broke off the conversation and turned himself away!'

'Had the answer,' he goes on to say, 'been such as William had looked for, and *might naturally have expected*, there is good reason for supposing that Episcopacy in this country might have retained its hold, and *that Scotland would have been Episcopalian at the present day.*'

Now, to what extent the policy of William was affected by the attitude of the bishops we do not pretend to be able to say. That it was affected in a measure is certain. The Prince of Orange was not likely to be drawn very cordially toward men who, just two days before he landed at Torbay, could write to King James as follows. After speaking of him as 'the darling of heaven,' and as having been 'miraculously prospered with glory and victory,' they say: 'We are amazed to hear of the danger of an invasion from Holland, which excites our prayers for an universal repentance from all orders of men that God may yet spare His people, preserve your royal person, and give such success to your Majesty's arms that all who invade your Majesty's just and undoubted rights may be disappointed and clothed with shame; so that on your royal head the crown may flourish.'

A document like that, with which William was no doubt made acquainted, was likely enough to be considered when the question of a policy came to be the subject of debate; and if the Prince interpreted Dr. Rose's innocent-looking sentence as an intimation that the Scottish Episcopate meant to continue the friends of James, he is assuredly not to be blamed in viewing them with distrust.

How far this behaviour of the bishops, however, determined the character of the new ecclesiastical establishment, is a question which is not so easily answered; and Dr. Wordsworth goes very far indeed beyond the record, when he assumes that there were no considerations but the petulance of Dr. Rose which influenced so astute a statesman as the Prince of Orange in coming to the conclusions which he reached.

4. **A Possible Episcopal Establishment.**—The truth is—and we say it emphatically—that if William had resolved to follow in the line of the Restoration, and had continued to give all the countenance of the State to the Episcopacy which the Stuarts had set up, not only would he and his immediate successors have found the government of Scotland a more difficult business than they did, but the Scottish Episcopal Church would itself have been made to occupy, in the eye of the world, a very much less reputable position than it does at this present hour.

We do not dwell on the political consequences of having not merely the Highlanders, but the Covenanters in opposition. What is of more interest to us here, is the question what would have been the religious and ecclesiastical effect of such an arrangement as Dr. Wordsworth conceives to have been possible.

If Dr. Rose, he says, had only been wiser, 'Scotland might have been Episcopalian at the present day.'

Suppose that that had come true—in what estimation, we ask, would an Episcopal Established Church have been held which had had such a history? We sometimes meet, even yet, with large assertions as to the number of people in Scotland who at the Revolution were to be found contentedly waiting on the ministrations of the curates. If a plebiscite of the inhabitants had been taken then, perhaps (it is suggested) the vote might have been for the maintenance of things as they were. Perhaps it might. The thing at least is not absolutely inconceivable. But can it ever be forgotten how such a thing had come to be possible? For six-and-twenty years, that is, for nearly a whole generation, the country had lain under the heel of the oppressor. By the operation of cruel laws, enforced with remorseless rigour, the natural leaders of the people had been either exterminated or banished. Four hundred of the nine hundred who composed the ministry of the Church at the Restoration were driven from their parishes, and their places filled by men who (their own friends being the witnesses) were ill qualified to keep alive the sparks of spiritual life. The population of Scotland was not then a third of what it is now, yet to secure for Prelacy even such a footing as it had in 1688, the blood of eighteen thousand persons required to be shed. Under circumstances like these, the marvel is not that Presbyterianism, but that *religion* itself, survived. And if, when all was done and a new order of things was being introduced, a fresh establishment of the Episcopal Church had taken place, a moral enormity would have been committed, under which that Church itself would in the long run have sunk.

Scottish Episcopacy may or may not be now an object of respect to the Scottish people (it will always be difficult for us to forget the crimes which were done in its name), but Scottish Episcopacy, such as Bishop Wordsworth would have had continued among us, would have been a system whose history no honourable Episcopalian could have read without shame. The seldomer, indeed, that they recall the fact that their Church was once established, the more hopeful will be their own prospects. Their progress must proceed from what they possess of present light and truth, not from the inspiring influence of their traditions. Prelacy was never chosen freely by the Scottish people. Whenever it was introduced, it was thrust upon them by secular authority. Once and again it was cast out, as intolerable, by popular uprisings,—showing always how the current tended to flow, when it was left to take its own course. And if at the Revolution the country had been really dragooned, as the Bishop of St. Andrews believes it was, into submitting to the system quietly, we can only say that the fact is a disgraceful one, which no Christian Church could take the benefit of, and hope to prosper. It would have been a practical embodiment and exhibition of iniquity rewarded.

5. **Principal Carstares.**—William was just as able as we are now to take a conjunct view of all the circumstances; and we may depend upon it, it was not merely the inconsiderate speech of Dr. Rose which determined him to pursue the line of policy which he took.

It was fortunate for him that he had at this juncture an adviser who was very well acquainted with Scottish affairs. This was William Carstares, afterwards Principal of the University of Edinburgh,—whose life and times have been described in a very able and interesting way by Dr. Story of Rosneath.

The father of the Principal was minister of the Cathedral Church, Glasgow, when the restoration of Charles II. took place, and he was one of the four hundred who were ejected from their parishes in 1662, when the Act was passed requiring submission to the bishops. John Carstares, the outed minister, led a fugitive life ever after, and as one of the consequences, his son William was sent for his education, not to any of the Scotch Universities, but to Utrecht in Holland. It was while he was there as a student that he was first introduced to the Prince of Orange. The two men took to one another. In course of time Carstares became one of William's chaplains, and it was he who proposed and conducted the thanksgiving service which the Dutch army of invasion engaged in when it first mustered on the shores of England.

In Dr. Story's opinion, William's policy was regulated by purely selfish considerations, and he thinks it quite possible that he might have committed the fatal mistake into which Dr. Wordsworth regrets now he did not fall, if it had not been for the fuller knowledge and wiser counsels of Carstares.

'To William,' he says, 'at Whitehall, Scotch Presbyterianism did not appear so potent an element in national life as to William at the Hague. During the twenty-eight years of its enforced suppression, Presbytery had undeniably dwindled in numbers and in influence. William, who was a Broad Churchman, or "Latitudinarian" (as the phrase ran in his own day), looked upon forms of Church government with indifference; and while prepared to tolerate all, was inclined to give the sanction of national establishment to those only which were upheld by supporters of his own authority. A thorough Erastian, he would yield no recognition to dogmatic or hierarchic pretensions, which were advanced by the avowed opponents of his Government and policy. While tolerating all sections of the Church, he would help to establish that one, and that only, which he understood would be most in harmony with his own Government and with the wishes of the people. He would not maintain a Church hostile to himself. He would not impose one hateful to the people. With these principles, the ecclesiastical settlement of Scotland perplexed him.' 'His finessing with the Episcopalians,' Dr. Story goes on to say, 'must have been disapproved by Carstares,' who warned him to 'beware of the Episcopal party,' and who drew up a paper which he entitled 'Hints to the King,' and in which he set forth cogent reasons why he ought to look to the Presbyterians. Among the reasons there given were these: That they (the Presbyterians) constituted 'the great body of the nation,'—that they were almost to a man in favour of the Revolution,—and that 'the Episcopal clergy in Scotland, particularly the prelates, had been so accustomed to warp their religious tenets with the political doctrines of regal supremacy, passive obedience, and non-resistance, that it would be inconsistent with the very end of his coming to continue Episcopacy upon its present footing in Scotland.'

These considerations prevailed, and under the Revolution Settlement the Episcopacy, which had been so imperiously imposed by Charles, was set aside, and Presbytery established in its room.

6. **Reconstitution of Presbytery.**—'The first step towards the reconstitution of the Presbyterian Establishment [we again quote Dr. Story] was the abolition of the Act of 1669, which

had made the King supreme over all persons, and in all causes, civil and ecclesiastical.'

The next was to restore the surviving ministers, about sixty, who had been ejected for not conforming to Episcopacy after the Restoration.

Then came the last and decisive measure which established the Church on the basis of the Confession of Faith, and of the Presbyterian polity as defined and secured by the Act of 1592.

Such were the leading points in the measure; but many other details followed, including the repeal of a long list of laws in favour of Episcopacy, the legalizing of the 'Rabbling of the Curates,' and the vesting of the government of the Church in the surviving ministers of 1662.

It was not possible, however, to carry through such a transformation in the then condition of Scotland in a perfectly satisfactory manner. William himself was an Erastian, as we have heard, and although he had more sense and breadth of mind than Charles, he had just as little respect for the Church as a divine institution; and although it would be most ungrateful to forget our obligations to Carstares, his biographer makes it very plain that he was not a man of the stamp of Melville and Henderson. The air of Holland and of the Court had broadened him, and he was able to make light of difficulties which would have seemed insuperable to his persecuted father. In such hands a policy of compromise was sure to be pursued.

At the same time, it must be admitted that, with the materials to be manipulated, there could have been no hope of anything like a peaceful arrangement, if an attempt had been made to construct an ideally perfect Establishment. A statesman of a later age might perhaps have thought of cutting the knot which it was so difficult to untie. He might have suggested the disendowing of all the sects, and the leaving of each to make its own way in the world. But that was an idea which, we are sure, occurred then to no one. And in contemplating a readjustment on a national basis, we are not surprised that it was deemed necessary to make concessions which are now known to have had mischievous consequences.

For example, no notice was taken of those COVENANTS to the inspiring influence of which Scotland owed in those days the preservation of her liberties.

Then, how much there is of fatal significance in this account of Carstares' attitude towards the Episcopal clergy and toward patronage!

'He dreaded,' says M'Cormick, 'the consequences which might ensue from entrusting the whole government of the Church and the disposal of the benefices in the hands of a set of men who were tainted with all the prejudices of the people, and at the same time irritated by a sense of recent injuries. While he advised, therefore, the establishment of Presbytery, he was of opinion that it ought to be of the most moderate kind, and so modelled as to admit of the assumption of such of the Episcopal clergy as took the oaths of Government upon the mildest terms. This he foresaw would not be the case unless the rights of patrons were preserved as a check upon the clergy.'

In conformity with these views, a middle measure was adopted in regard to patronage. The voice of the people was recognised as a potential element in the settlement of ministers, but the right of nomination was conferred on the heritors and elders; while as to the curates, so easy a place of repentance was made for them, that a considerable number found no difficulty in remaining in their parishes after the Revolution as Presbyterian ministers.

7. **Rabbling the Curates.**—Reference has been made to the 'Rabbling of the Curates.' This is how the action of the populace is described when, in at least 200 parishes, the inhabitants took the law into their own hands at the Revolution, and summarily dismissed the Episcopal ministers who had been intruded upon them. Dr. Wordsworth is shocked at the levity with which Dr.

Story comments on these outrages. They occurred in the winter. They were inflicted on clergymen who had been ordained by bishops. The poor men were driven out of their homes with their wives and children, and 'often without the means of shelter and of livelihood.' And in the eye of the Bishop of St. Andrews, their wrongs were equal to those of the hunted Covenanter. Dr. Story has no patience with this abuse of sentiment and of history. 'Never,' says he, 'were enormous wrongs so leniently retaliated. Never in the day when power had passed from the oppressors to the oppressed, was the oppression so lightly revenged.'

The conduct of the rabble is, of course, not to be justified. Men have no business to take the law into their own hands. But when Episcopalians in these times are showing a revived inclination to 'bleat and whimper' over incidents which speak at once for the suppressed indignation of the people during the continuance of the prelatic *régime*, and for their self-command when it came to an end, they would do well to listen to the remonstrance of an English contemporary writer who had personally examined into the whole matter of Presbyterian persecutions, and who writes as follows :—

'I would advise the gentlemen that talk of this as part of the persecutions they complain of, to leave *it* out of the list, and let it lie as an accident of the Revolution, and as an effect of the rage of a provoked people, in which religion had no share. . . . If they did not pistol in cold blood ; if they did not tie women to stakes in the sea and let the tide flow over them ; if they did not drag you out of your houses and shoot you without giving you time to commend your souls to God's mercy,—if these things were not done, you ought to believe that none of the posterity of these poor innocents that so suffered were alive to revenge them, or that you had more mercy from their hands than you had reason to expect.'

Such a style of arguing will have no effect on minds like that of Dr. Wordsworth. He deliberately contends that the opposition of the Covenanters to Prelacy was probably '*more offensive to God than the commission of cruelty and persecution!*' and to him, therefore, the expulsion of the curates seems a supreme act of sacrilege. But common sense will assert itself in defiance of priestly pretensions, and few intelligent laymen, even of the Episcopal communion, will have much difficulty in excusing this lawless but natural uprising of the people.

8. **Weak Indulgence.**—Apart from the rabbling of the curates, the Presbyterians were indulgent to the verge of indifference. Whether they were cowed by the persecutions to which they had been subjected, or whether the strength of William's iron hand was made so sensible as to overpower all thought of opposition, certain it is that they lay almost passive in the hands of the Government and its advisers, and submitted with scarcely a struggle to whatever arrangement was considered to be for their good. So far from the Prelatists, after the Revolution, having cause to complain that toleration was not extended to them, the author of the old pamphlet[1] to which reference has been made, and who is shrewdly suspected to have been no other than Defoe himself, says : 'By the Act of 1695, it was taken quite out of the power of the Church to depose any man merely for being Episcopal in principle, or for refusing to own the Presbyterian Church. Nay, the Episcopal clergy, who by virtue of this Act remain in their livings many of them to this day, refuse to acknowledge the Church, to submit to any of her judicatories, or to join either in discipline or worship. And yet in all their affronts of the Established Church they continue in their parishes preaching and using all their formalities, however contrary to the inclinations and desires of the people, *who in some places are fain to set up meeting-houses in their parishes, and be at the charge of entertaining a Presbyterian minister as a Dissenter to preach to them, because they cannot bear the fopperies and opposition of their parish minister.*'

[1] *Presbyterian Persecution Examined,* etc.

9. **The Revolution Church.**—The Church of the Revolution, then, was in no sense a very strong one. Its ministry was composed, *first*, of sixty elderly men, the survivors of the ejectment of 1662; *second*, of more than a hundred others who had been ordained afterwards, but who had many of them conformed in various ways to the prelatic system; *third*, of the three preachers who had been ministering among the hill-folk or extreme Covenanters; and *lastly*, of the curates who were found willing to submit to the new order of things. The Presbyterian element was the strongest in this variously compounded body, because its representatives had most principle, and had the countenance, besides, at once of the masses and of the State. But it was easy to predict that nothing but a miracle could make its course peaceful and prosperous. If in the earlier Assemblies it showed itself honestly desirous of benefiting the country, it was unmistakably timid in the execution of its plans; and not many years had passed before that Moderate party began to take shape from which not much good has come to Scotland.

Its chief sources of danger were within. But outside also there were various things which bore a threatening aspect. It may be a question whether the Cameronians did not serve a better purpose by standing aloof than they would have done by conforming. If they had allowed themselves to be absorbed, they might soon have been assimilated. In any case, though they insisted on fighting under their own flag, we cannot think of them but as friends of the Church. It was different, however, with the Papists, who had increased in number and influence under James (some of the leading Scottish politicians having become perverts), — and with the Prelatists, who in certain localities constituted the mass of the people. These received support from many of the landowners; and as they were mainly Jacobites praying secretly for the Pretender over the water, they proved a disturbing element in the country, not merely religiously, but politically. We frankly admit that we do not see very clearly how those who had the making of the time could have done very differently from what they did. But let us distinctly understand where the blame of the complications of that age properly lies. To get at the spring of the evil we must go back to the Restoration, and to the unprincipled counsels of the founder of modern Scottish Episcopacy — Archbishop Sharp. We have often to make the best of things when they have got so hopelessly ravelled that they cannot be put perfectly to rights; but in submitting to what has become a necessity, it may be both lawful and right to remember who is responsible for having brought us into trouble. If Scotland had been left in 1660 to follow its own light instead of having Prelacy thrust upon it, its history would have been very different from what it became.

1. *In what respects were Charles and James like and unlike each other?*
2. *What claim had William to the throne?*
3. *When did the Prince of Orange land in England?*
4. *What became of the King?*
5. *How did the Bishops act?*
6. *What might have happened if they had been more prudent?*
7. *In what light would an Episcopal Establishment have appeared to posterity?*
8. *Who was Carstares?*
9. *Describe his character.*
10. *For what are we indebted to him?*
11. *State the steps taken in reconstituting Presbytery.*
12. *Can the rabbling of the curates be excused?*
13. *Wherein lay the weakness of the Revolution Establishment?*
14. *Describe the state of things in Scotland after the Settlement.*

CHAPTER IX.

THE SECESSIONS.

THE first event which affected seriously the position of the Church after the Revolution was the Union of England and Scotland, in 1707. For several years previously that consummation was foreshadowed; and in various Acts of Assembly passed about that time, one can trace symptoms showing that what was coming was regarded with apprehension. Though the King and the politicians of the period ignored the Covenants, these were not quite forgotten by the Church, and their influence is visible in the anxiety displayed for the revival of spiritual religion and for the preservation of the Presbyterian form of government. The importance of such an incident, therefore, as the suppression of the Scottish Parliament could not be overlooked, and if the advantages of the proposed measure were admitted, its disadvantages were also recognised to an extent which made its acceptance by the more earnest Churchmen by no means cordial.

1. **The Good and Evil of the Union.**—We can now see still more clearly the good of the Union and the evil of it. It took away from Jacobitism much of its power to do mischief. It increased the material prosperity of Scotland. It made the government of the whole country easier and more orderly. But, on the other hand, it deprived the Scottish nation of much of its legitimate influence in the regulation of its internal affairs, and it not only drew to London our upper classes, but (by the operation of the sacramental test and otherwise) led to that abandon-

ment by them of their own national Church, which is to this hour one of the most perilous and unsatisfactory of our social characteristics.

The strength of the anxiety felt about the possible evil of the Union is revealed in the care which was taken to secure the liberties of the Church.

An Act of Security was passed by which the Confession of Faith and the Presbyterian form of Church government were ratified and established 'to continue without any alteration to the people of this land in all succeeding generations;' and it was further declared that this Act of Security, 'with the establishment therein contained, shall be held and observed in all time coming as a fundamental and essential condition of any treaty of Union to be concluded betwixt the two kingdoms, without any alteration thereof or derogation thereto in any sort for ever.'

The Articles of Union as ultimately adopted included these conditions, and the Scottish Church made a fresh start under the new *régime*, carrying with her the comfortable assurance that she was as safe from encroachment on the side of England as the most stringent statute law could make her.

2. **Restoration of Patronage.**—It was really a devout imagination to suppose that any such bonds could be binding for all time. A nation must lay its account with changing somewhat in the course of centuries, and it was an unreasonable assumption to make, that the Revolution Establishment was so perfect as to be incapable of improvement 'in any sort for ever.' But while that may be conceded, it would be difficult to find terms strong enough to denounce, as it deserves, the shameful breach of faith of which the English Parliament was guilty, when in 1712—just five years after it had become solemnly bound to let the Scottish Church alone—it summarily, and in the face of earnest remonstrances from all parties in the Church, set aside the Act of Security, and restored lay patronage.

It is difficult to account for this apparently gratuitous assault upon the Scottish Church, but by supposing that it was an outcome of one of the political plots of the period. It is certain that at this time the party in power in England had strong Jacobite leanings ; and the measure may have been intended to serve Jacobite ends. It seems rather an extreme idea to suggest that they hoped to break up the Union by showing how utterly valueless were its securities. But it is not unlikely that they had it in their heart to weaken the influence of the Presbyterian Church by making it less popular in its constitution, and bringing it more under aristocratic control.

What moved them to aim at that object was not merely that the Church was politically opposed to them, but that they wished to give an impulse to the Episcopal party, on whose active partisanship they could depend. The Act of Toleration, which was passed in 1711, is one with whose provisions we cannot but now agree. It allowed nonconforming congregations to establish themselves anywhere, and to use the Anglican Liturgy if they pleased. It also exempted their members from submission to the Presbyterian judicatories. But while the new laws were in themselves unobjectionable, they were straws showing how the winds were blowing. 'The Church,' says Dr. Story, 'had, even long before the Union, dreaded that those who sought to undermine her would make a joint attack through toleration and the restoration of patronage ; nor did the Episcopal and Jacobite party pretend to hide their designs of undoing that portion of the treaty which solemnly secured the perpetual establishment of the Presbyterian Church.' Carstares saw through their designs more clearly, perhaps, than any one else, and his doing so explains what has puzzled those who claim him as the founder of the Moderate party, that, latitudinarian though he was, he led the opposition both against the Act of Toleration and the restoration of patronage.

3. **The Consequences.**—The unprincipled conduct of the British

Parliament in 1712 was historically parallel to that of Charles II. in 1660. The latter imperiously imposed upon the Scottish Church a form of government at which it revolted. The former, in an equally imperious way, imposed upon it a system which was intensely distasteful to it, and in open defiance of its formal and solemn protests. What happened as the result of the restoration of Episcopacy has been told in the story of the persecutions. What followed from the restoration of patronage was the breaking up of the Church into innumerable fragments.

At first Queen Anne's Act was almost a dead letter. For the settlement of a minister in a parish, there were needed, not merely the patron's presentation, but the call of the people and the concurrence of the presbytery of the bounds, and for some time—so unpopular was the new arrangement—few probationers would accept a patron's nomination. But some astute landowners began to make capital out of this excessive conscientiousness. When a vacancy occurred, they named in connection with it men who they knew would not accept their invitation, and time was thus lost to their own material gain. For although the parishes were left unsupplied with ordinances, the patrons appropriated the stipend. The Church could not see such a state of things continued, and it interfered. But it was little it could do to rectify the great wrong which had been committed. Petitions to Parliament—protests in the Assembly—deputations to London, were all resorted to in vain. Patronage was restored, and it had to be submitted to. And so, after a good deal of exclamation and struggling, things were allowed, so far as formal ecclesiastical action was concerned, to settle down.

What happened in consequence is well known. Patrons became bolder in the exercise of their 'rights.' Probationers grew to be less scrupulous in accepting appointments. And before the middle of the century, it had come to be recognised by the majority as an indisputably wise practical policy to give full effect to every legally drawn presentation at all hazards. Such a consummation was not reached, of course, without friction. The people could not anywhere see the 'call' set aside without dissatisfaction. And many a presbytery must have winced under the operations of the Riding Committees, and the still more tyrannical law of the Assembly, which left them no individual liberty in cases of the most unwarrantable intrusion. But it is undeniable that the great mass of the ministry must have acquiesced in this silent revolution, and the simple fact of such an acquiescence—so speedy and so complete—goes a long way to explain the secessions which began to take place within twenty years after patronage had been restored.

4. **Causes of the Separation.**—The popular belief is that the Erskines and Gillespie were driven out of the Church simply because they came to adopt views which were regarded as incompatible with their position about the rights of the Christian people. That was certainly one of the causes of their expulsion, but it was by no means the only cause or the deepest cause. The truth is, that the Church to begin with was constituted of discordant elements, which could only have held together for any considerable length of time if the comprehensionist principle, which now prevents the Church of England from falling to pieces, had been then known and allowed to operate. In the Erskines one sees, under changed circumstances, the successors of the Covenanters; and their struggle, though not against Prelacy enforced by the sabres of dragoons, was just as truly for Presbytery and Liberty and Evangelism. Had the Moderates, who very soon gained the ascendancy, been as wise and temperate as their modern vindicators say they were, they might, by the exercise of a very small amount of tolerance, have at least delayed the catastrophe. New wine and old may be kept in the same bottle, if the stopper is judiciously removed. And if the representatives of the ancient witnesses had only been left free to testify against the corruptions which they saw around them, and to exempt

themselves from personal complicity in acts which they condemned, the dissolution of the Revolution Establishment would not have begun so early. But there seems to have been no large-minded apprehension of the true character of the situation. The two great 'schools' of which the Church was composed became conscious of their essential antagonism. The Evangelicals were in a minority, but, confident in the goodness of their cause, they were zealous and uncompromising. On the other hand, the Moderates came to ascertain their numerical strength. They were annoyed by the religious pretensions of their opponents, which appeared to reflect upon themselves. And being no doubt honestly persuaded that the policy of encouraging 'the democracy' was an unwise one, they set about such measures of repression as promised to issue in at least an outward uniformity. In this attempt to give unity to the Church they could not draw upon the secular arm, as their predecessors had done, but they had considerable spiritual resources, and these they employed, if not wisely, yet with vigour.

5. **Questions of Doctrine.**—The 'persecution' which now began was inaugurated by an attack upon the *doctrine* of the minority. An English book, called *The Marrow of Modern Divinity*, was reissued in Scotland by Mr. James Hog of Carnock, who wrote for it a commendatory preface. The theology of the Book is not different from that taught in our Standards, but the General Assembly of 1720 was persuaded by Principal Haddow of St. Andrews that it was unsound, and an Act was passed condemning its propagators, and placing the work in an *Index Expurgatorius*. These proceedings brought to the front twelve men, among whom were Ebenezer Erskine and Thomas Boston, who felt that the truth of God and the faith of the Church were condemned in their condemnation. They did what they could by discussions and representations to have the matter set right, but without a great deal of success. The Act, indeed, was explained so far; but the complainants were summoned for

their pains to appear at the bar of the Assembly, and to receive there a solemn rebuke for their meddlesomeness, and for avowed sympathy with 'heresy.'

6. **Toleration on the Left.**—While Evangelicalism was thus dealt with so imperiously, a more notorious case showed how far the Moderate party were prepared to go in tolerating aberrations on *the Left*. Professor Simson of Glasgow was accused of holding and teaching Arian doctrines; yet it was with the greatest difficulty that the Assembly could be induced to remove him from his chair. This readiness to repress men of the type of Boston and to shield men of the type of Simson, was significant as a symptom of the time, and in it we are to see another of the causes which forced on the collision.

7. **Repression of the People.**—No case of intrusion into a parish against the will of the people took place till 1725. But soon after that date such cases began to occur with increasing frequency,—and here the fatal folly of the Moderate majority was displayed in a way which inevitably precipitated the rupture which was approaching.

That the people were intended to occupy a potential place even under the Act of Queen Anne, is undeniable. They had the right to adhibit or refuse to adhibit their names to a 'call.' But the secularizing influence of patronage had now told, and the leaders of the majority had arrived at the conclusion that the call was a formality which might be disregarded. Every presentee, therefore, was forced into the charge to which he was nominated, whether the parishioners concurred or not; and when presbyteries happened to be recalcitrant, the Assembly took the matter into its own hands and settled the objectionable man by a committee of its own.

But this was not all. The authorities not only committed these enormities, but refused to listen to any remonstrances. A representation signed by forty ministers was addressed to the Assembly of 1732, but it was not even allowed to be read. When Ebenezer Erskine preached before the Synod of Stirling a sermon in which he proclaimed the need for reform, he was sharply called to account. And on Erskine's refusing to submit to a rebuke, he was first suspended, and then separated from his charge.

8. **Erskine and Gillespie.**—It was this crowning act of tyranny which led to the first Secession. Erskine was joined by three other ministers—Fisher of Kinclaven, Wilson of Perth, and Moncreiff of Abernethy—in protesting against the intolerance of the Moderate majority. All the four, having elected to make common cause together, were treated in the same manner. Being driven, unjustifiably as all now believe, out of the ministry, they not unnaturally took the further step of going out of the Church. On the 6th December 1733 they constituted themselves into an Associated Presbytery; and thus began to flow the little runlet which has now swollen into a formidable flood.

For a time the parties who had brought about this catastrophe were alarmed at the consequences of their policy, and they went a very long way to make amends to the brethren whom they had offended, in the hope of bringing them back. But when all their efforts proved vain they desisted, and within a wonderfully short period we find them not only following their old counsels, but pursuing these more recklessly than ever.

A Riding Committee might not have been an admirable institution in itself, but it was an immense convenience. When a presbytery could not see its own way to induct an unacceptable presentee into a parish, it had only to roll the responsibility over upon the Assembly, and that venerable court was always able to find agents to do its work. The arrangement, however, was not an orderly one; and there is something to be said for Principal Robertson, who seriously objected to it, and got the Church to agree that each presbytery must be required to transact its own business. But here again a fresh illustration was furnished of the incurable viciousness of the system. Mr. Gillespie of Carnock could not bring his mind to assent to the settlement of Mr. Brown of Inverkeithing. In the days of the Riding Committee the Presbytery of Dunfermline could have managed without him. But Dr. Robertson's new rule had come into force, and he could not be spared. Of the two alternatives before him, he chose to obey his conscience rather than his ecclesiastical superiors, and was deposed for contumacy. The experience gave him a new view of patronage. It seemed to him now a burden which no Church could bear and prosper; and though with a heart full of loyalty to the Church of Scotland, he was driven to become the founder of another sect, which indicated his attitude to succeeding generations by taking to itself the name of the Relief Church. Thomas Boston, the author of *The Fourfold State*, did not live long enough to take part in either Secession; but his son, who became minister of Jedburgh, joined Mr. Gillespie, and they two with an elder made the first Relief Presbytery. Mr. Gillespie was deposed in 1752.

These events may be very deplorable, but they are very intelligible. In reading the life of Carstares, the real organizer of the Revolution Church, one is struck with his sagacity and fairmindedness. We repeat again what we have already said: That if there was to be a national Establishment at all, the Establishment constituted was the only one which could very reasonably have been set up. But Carstares must have been a very sanguine man indeed, if he believed that he had so adjusted the elements which he found existing as to make a speedy explosion improbable. These elements were kept for a time in a state of quiescence by outward pressure; but they could not amalgamate, and they could not agree to differ. It is vain to speculate what would have happened if the Covenanting section of the Church had gained the ascendancy. What really took place was, that the leaven prevailed which owed its origin to the teaching of the curates. That, with the characteristic intolerance of the time, made a breach inevitable. The Erskines and others were happily not driven, as their fathers were, to the mountains and moors. Liberty of worship, for which a past generation had fought in vain, was now conceded fully. But the persecuting spirit still lived in the tyrannical majority, which denied to conscientious men even the relief of protest—and as a refuge from that there was no resource but *Secession*.

1. What was the first important public event after the Revolution?
2. Indicate the good and evil of it.
3. What steps were taken to secure the liberty of the Church?
4. How was the Act of Security maintained?
5. What was the Act of Toleration?
6. What motives led to the restoration of Patronage?
7. What is the popular view of the cause of the Secessions?
8. How are they really to be accounted for?
9. About what book did a difference of opinion arise?
10. Who supported and opposed it?
11. In what direction was toleration shown?
12. How were the people treated?
13. Indicate the immediate causes of the Secessions.
14. Give the dates of both.
15. In what way may it be said that they were inevitable?

CHAPTER X.

THE ERA OF MODERATISM.

WITH the turn of the century there rose into notice a man who at the time was only a country minister, but who for nearly thirty years after 1752 ruled the Assembly with the authority of a dictator. Principal Robertson was not the first of the Moderate 'leaders.' The era of 'Moderatism' began (Principal Tulloch thinks) in 1720, and then Principal Haddow reigned. Dr. Robertson also had as his immediate predecessor Dr. Cuming, who was a Moderate to all intents and purposes. But there are many considerations which move us to date the period of which we are now to speak from 1752. In the first place, for example, between 1720 and the middle of the century, the conflict between the two parties in the Church was waged with such vigour on the one side and such hesitation on the other, that the question who was to gain in the end was a matter of at least considerable uncertainty. When the first Secession took place, in 1732, a feeling of serious alarm sprang up, and so many concessions were made to the Erskines and their friends, that it looked, for a time, as if the Assembly were really altering its course, and proposing to proceed on a new tack altogether. It by and by recovered its spirits again, and went on as formerly; but Dr. Cuming himself was opposed to patronage, and was extremely averse to putting upon scrupulous brethren, in connection with disputed settlements, a heavier burden than they could bear.

Besides, for another thing, it was in 1742 that those remarkable spiritual movements began, in Cambuslang and Kilsyth, which brought Whitefield himself down to Scotland, and by which the whole Church must, in some degree, have been stirred. Before the middle of the century was reached there had occurred a subsidence of the tide. But it is difficult to realize that the full triumph of Moderatism had been achieved while revivals like these were in progress.

The crisis was reached when Mr. Robertson of Gladsmuir, seconded by Mr. Home, the author of the tragedy of *Douglas*, succeeded in persuading the Assembly to pay no heed either to the popular will in connection with ministerial vacancies, or to the conscientious scruples of presbyteries who had reclaiming congregations to face. The law, it was now held, gave to patrons the right to nominate whom they pleased to vacant cures, and no man had any liberty save to give legal effect to their presentations.

We shall learn something of the era which now began from the character of its leading spirit.

1. **Character of Robertson.**—He was a man after Dean Stanley's own heart. Personally he was most attractive, and although 'it is difficult for us, with the advances made since his time, fully to comprehend what he did for history,' we can all appreciate the fact that in his day he took a first place among men of letters as the historian of Scotland, of America, and of Charles V.

'His first appearance,' says the Dean, 'was as a young minister in the General Assembly, when he at once led them captive by his eloquence. From that time for twenty years he remained its complete master. His administration was remarkable as showing how complete independence of worldly influence may be combined with complete vindication of the superiority of law to ecclesiastical caprices. He insisted on the same strictness in the judicial proceedings of the Assembly as was observed in the other courts of justice, and left behind him a series of decisions which were long venerated as a kind of common law in Scotland.

'He was also,' adds Dr. Stanley, 'as thorough a latitudinarian as Leighton.'

The eloquent speech above referred to was the one which led to the deposition of Mr. Gillespie of Carnock, and to the formation of the Relief Church; and Dr. Robertson, in vindicating 'the superiority of law to ecclesiastical caprices,'—that is, in giving effect to all legal presentations at whatever hazard,—covered the country with Secession meeting-houses. But if the Dean knew these facts, he did not consider it material to make any mention of them. Robertson's 'comprehensive grasp,' 'his learning,' 'his dignity,' his influence as 'the mighty Churchman who ruled the Church of Scotland as no one had done since the death of Carstares,' these are the things which filled the Dean's eye and stirred his admiration. And he did not think it worth his while to turn aside, even for a moment, to ask whether the policy which was the outcome of them all had stood the test of time and of experience.

But there are others who have studied the character of Dr. Robertson—looking at him from a different standpoint. Here, for example, is how the great Scottish Churchman appeared to William Wilberforce when he was taking his *Practical View of Christianity*. Having in the text of his book expressed great regret 'that many of the most eminent of the *literati* of modern times have been professed unbelievers, and that others of them have discovered such lukewarmness in the cause of Christ as to treat with especial goodwill and attention and respect those men who, by their avowed publications, were openly assailing or insidiously undermining the very foundations of the Christian hope—considering themselves as more closely united to them by literature than severed from them by the widest religious differences, Wilberforce adds in a note :—'It is with pain that the author finds himself compelled to place so great a writer as Dr. Robertson in this [second] class. But to say nothing of his phlegmatic account of the Reformation . . . his letters to Mr. Gibbon, lately published, cannot but excite emotions of regret and shame in every sincere Christian.'

Robertson, as we have heard, was 'a thorough latitudinarian, and as 'toleration is a plant of easy growth in the soil of indifference,' he felt no difficulty in associating on the most intimate terms with David Hume, or in speaking generously about all differences in religious belief. But, if we are to credit Dr. Carlyle of Inveresk, he took part in what looks like a conspiracy to break down the manners of his time as well as the strictness of its faith. 'There were a few of us,' says Dr. Carlyle, 'who, besides the natural levity of youth and the natural freedom of our manners, *had an express design* to throw contempt on that vile species of hypocrisy which magnified an indecorum into a crime, and gave an air of false sanctimony and Jesuitism to the greatest part of the clergy, and was thereby pernicious to rational religion.' The conspiracy so far succeeded. 'We freed the clergy from many unreasonable and hypocritical restraints.' But there were lengths to which the leaders of the Church dared not go.

Drs. Robertson and Blair, though they both visited the great actress [Mrs. Siddons] in private, often regretted to me that they had not seized the opportunity which was given them by her superior talents and unexceptionable character of going openly to the theatre, which would have put an end to all future animadversions on the subject.'

These notes may suffice to give some idea of the man. That the religious side of his nature came out in a more attractive way in his intercourse with confidential friends, we can scarcely doubt when we remember what was said about him by his colleague, Dr. Erskine. But looking at his public life and his policy as a leader, it is plain that his influence must have been injurious in many ways.

It was at a terrible cost to the Church that he 'vindicated the superiority of law to ecclesiastical caprices.' His own readiness to make greater allowance for Hume and Gibbon than for the Seceders, could not but have a relaxing effect on the faith of the country. And although he did not actually set the fashion of clerical attendance on the theatre, his confidential communications to Dr. Carlyle must have helped materially to the toleration of freer modes of life.

Now the character of Robertson is reflected in his age.

2. **Policy of Intrusion.**—It was not all at once or without a struggle that 'the ecclesiastical caprices' of the Scottish people suffered themselves to be repressed. When a vacancy occurred in a parish, the inhabitants would insist that they had some interest in the man who was to be their new spiritual teacher, and they sometimes opposed themselves to a presentee very energetically. But the law, as interpreted by Dr. Robertson, refused to give way. It asserted itself, in fact, now and again with the help of a troop of dragoons. And it came to be by no means an unheard of thing to make 'a desolation and call it peace.' In 1756, for instance, Mr. Patrick Grant was settled 'to the walls of the Kirk at Nigg.' At Jedburgh the people left the Church *en masse,* and built a meeting-house for young Mr. Boston, the magistrates attending his induction services in their robes of office. That was in 1757. A still more famous, though a considerably later case, was that of St. Ninian's, where, in opposition to six hundred heads of families, sixty heritors, and all the elders but one, Mr. Thomson was ordained to be, as it was called, 'the stipend-lifter of the parish.' To bear up, however, against the weight of an overpowering authority was felt, in most cases, to be impossible; and in course of time the people settled down into sullen or indifferent acquiescence. Those who cared for religion left and joined the Seceders. Those who were ready to take things easily (and their number steadily increased) lost the little religion they had, and helped to form that great outlying mass of home heathenism with which we have ever since had to contend.

When one reads what were the material consequences of 'a steady and uniform support of the law of patronage,' one is surprised that the worldly wisdom for which Moderatism gets so much credit, did not earlier take alarm. Up to a certain date the funds placed at the disposal of the kirk-sessions were found sufficient for the support of the poor; but when the Seceders began to multiply, parochial assessments were soon found to be necessary.—And the depletion continued to proceed with such rapidity, that there was just cause for serious apprehensions in regard to the future. In 1774—just forty years after the first Secession—a calculation was made, which showed that at least one hundred and fifty congregations had sprung up outside the Establishment, and that the sum which had been expended on their maintenance could not have been less than £1,200,000. So large a sum taken out of a poor country in which there was supposed to be a national provision for gospel ordinances, represented a state of things which even political economists could not view with satisfaction.

3. **Doctrinal Laxity.**—The stringency of Dr. Robertson's ecclesiastical polity stood out in strong contrast to his laxity in relation to doctrine. He would concede nothing to the people, but he was wonderfully indulgent to his own order, the clergy. There was, indeed, a limit beyond which he would not go, even in that connection. Sir H. Moncreiff Wellwood expressly assures us that what at least confirmed the Principal in his determination to retire in 1780 from the leadership of the Assembly, was his aversion to a movement which he felt he could not control, the object of which was the abolition of the law requiring clerical subscription to the Confession of Faith. But if he refused to go that length, he by no means insisted on a practical conformity to the Confession; and a very uncertain sound indeed was now often heard from the pulpits of the Scottish Church.

The most famous preacher of the period was Blair. 'Neither of Tillotson nor of Jeremy Taylor in past times,' says Dean Stanley, 'nor of Arnold or Newman, or even Frederick Robertson in our own time, can it be recorded, as of Blair, that his sermons were translated into almost all the languages of Europe, and won for their author a public reward from the Crown.' And yet, the

Dean admits, these sermons are now forgotten. People still read Erskine, and Boston, and Rutherford, but the discourses —*auro magis aurei*, as Samuel Johnson called them—of Hugh Blair have gone for ever out of sight. Why? Obviously because so much of their force lay in their rhetoric. Their theology is, if we may say so, nowhere. There is little in them to meet the needs of sinners who have been moved to ask the way of life, or to guide awakened men through the perplexities and temptations of the world.

Robert Burns, whose own sympathies were anti-evangelical, but who quite understood the character of his time, had, we may believe, in his eye some imitator of Blair in the following description. The lines indicate clearly enough wherein lay at once the weakness and the strength of this order of moderate preaching—its elegance of form and its emptiness of Christian doctrine :—

> What signifies his barren shine
> Of moral powers and reason?
> His English style and gestures fine
> Are a' clean out of season.
> Like Socrates or Antonine,
> Or some old pagan heathen,
> The moral man he does define,
> But ne'er a word of faith in.
> That's right this day.

David Hume's humorous remark to Dr. Carlyle, after hearing him preach for their mutual friend the author of *Douglas*, illustrates in a similar way the condition of things at this time. 'What did you mean,' said he, 'by treating John's congregation to-day to one of Cicero's Academics? I did not think such heathen morality could have passed in East Lothian.'

Blair, however, represents very much only the negative side of Moderatism. The worst that can be said of his doctrine is, that there was so little of it. Morality is made to take the place of Christianity. But there followed him men whose religious teaching became more positive, and it was no uncommon thing to hear in ministerial circles an open denial of the supernatural.

There is hardly a district in the country which has not its traditions of ministers who lived and died in the Church of Scotland but were thorough Rationalists. The case of Mr. Nicoll of Traquair is a curious one. His sermons were actually published after his death for the express purpose of promoting Socinianism. And Dr. Scott of Carluke did even better service for his faith; for, when he was taken away, he left behind him in his parish the nucleus of a nonconforming Unitarian congregation. The corruption in doctrine sprang from the absence of life. In the Scottish Church of the eighteenth century there was no lack of activity. But the activity was not displayed within the sphere of spiritual religion. While a living stream of water will keep itself pure, we know what must happen with a pool in a state of stagnation.

4. **Freedom of Life.**—The indulgence extended to the doctrine of the clergy was made to embrace their conduct also. Dr. Carlyle, who, writing from the interior, is, of course, one of our great authorities on the subject of Moderatism, notes a significant feature in the character of Robertson's predecessor in the leadership, Dr. Patrick Cuming. 'He had,' says he, 'both learning and sagacity, and very agreeable conversation, *with a constitution able to bear the conviviality of the times.*' For the habits of their day the clergy were, of course, not exclusively responsible; but the times being what they were, social temptations were many, and there were not a few who succumbed to them. But the Church courts, which were severe to tyranny in the repression of popular discontent, were exceedingly tender in the exercise of discipline; and although no cases could reach the Assembly but such as were extraordinarily clamant, the instances of deposition or suspension for moral offences were as uncommon as for heresy.

5. **A Revolutionary Time.**—We have spoken of Principal Robertson's reign as marking the time when Moderatism culminated,

but it would be very unjust to lay at his door all the doubtful features of the period. A great many things contributed to make the latter half of the eighteenth century what it was. The breath of a new era was being felt over all Europe. In France especially there was being developed that impatience of the past, and of the existing, which broke out in the Revolution of 1789. The stir in men's minds which was experienced elsewhere, affected Scotland as well as other countries, and, the spell of the ancient religion being to a great extent broken, a portion of the *perfervidum ingenium* of the people naturally found expression in sympathy with the spirit of the age. If the country had been larger, the literary activity which so strikingly characterized the period might have been displayed outside the Church or without reference to it. At present it never occurs to us to think of the ecclesiastical connections of our poets, our historians, or our philosophers. But in Scotland, in the eighteenth century, the Church was very much coextensive with the nation, and whatever was then written had a bearing on it and an interest for it, which we can now hardly realize. Even Hume, sceptic though he was, hung about the vestibule. He did not give over attending public worship, nor did he cease to be on excellent terms with the leading ministers of the Church. And the same friendly intercourse was maintained with all the men who were trying to introduce from different quarters new light into the country.

Adam Smith published his work on the *Moral Sentiments* in 1750, and his *Wealth of Nations* in 1776. Hume composed his *Treatise on Human Nature* in France, and published it in 1734. The first of his Essays appeared in 1742, and his *Inquiry into the Principles of Morals* in 1752. Lord Kaimes, in the same year (1752), gave to the world his work on the *Principles of Morality and Natural Religion*. While Thomas Reid, the founder of the distinctively Scottish School of Philosophy, published his *Inquiry into the Human Mind on the Principles of Common Sense* in the year 1764. Reid began his public career as a parish minister,

His settlement in New Machar was very distasteful to the people, and he was indebted to Principal Robertson's high-handed law for his admission. But he overcame the opposition ultimately by his personal kindliness, and those who fought against his induction would in the end have fought to prevent his transference to Aberdeen. It is said of him by his biographer, Dugald Stewart, that he was so modest that he did not venture to preach his own sermons, but gave his people in their stead the better discourses of Tillotson and Evans!

Let the reader note the dates of the various books mentioned above. He will see that they are all embraced within the period of Dr. Robertson's leadership. And putting these two things together, —the evidence these works supply of the extraordinary mental activity which was then abroad, and the intimacy of the leading clergy with their authors,—it will at once be seen that, in order to understand the Church of the time, it is necessary to take into account not merely its internal and peculiarly ecclesiastical currents, but likewise the forces which were operating upon it from without. There can be no doubt in any case that the diversion of the clerical mind to non-professional studies, and the spirit of doubt and philosophical questioning which was abroad, told injuriously on the pulpit of the period. And one illustration of this is given by Dr. M'Kelvie in his *Annals of the United Presbyterian Church.* He names no fewer than thirty-five Secession congregations which resulted from the 'negative theology' of parochial clergymen.

6. **The Seceders.**—Meanwhile another stream with better elements in it was flowing and expanding over the country. The Secession, which started in 1733 with four congregations, had multiplied itself fifty-fold before the century ended. It, too, had had its tempestuous seasons. So early as 1749 there took place what was always pathetically spoken of afterwards as '*The Breach.*' Over what seems to us now a small point—the right reading of an oath required of burgesses—there arose a quarrel

which issued in disruption. The Church of the Erskines split into two—one section coming to be known as the Burgher, the other as the Anti-Burgher Synod. These two bodies coalesced again long afterwards,—in 1820,—and then adopted a new name, that of the *United Secession.* But many years before that last date each of the parts had suffered additional mutilation. The stir of the French Revolution, and the new ideas which were imported in connection with it, told not merely on the Establishment, but on those outside of it. The kind of effect, however, which was produced upon the Seceders was very different from that which was produced upon the Moderate clergy. Whatever was the *rationale* of it, the new epoch appears to have impelled many of them in the direction of those views of the spirituality of Christ's kingdom which ultimately developed into Voluntaryism. The drift of these novelties was not acceptable to all in either Synod. The Burghers and Anti-Burghers alike threw off fragments which claimed to retain the old light, and the new century began with this state of things,—the offshoot from the Revolution Church having undergone extraordinary extension on the whole, but internally weakened by discord and division.

This tendency to split up into fragments characterized the elder as well as the later Nonconformists. The Cameronians, or Reformed Presbyterians, did not always hang together any more than the Seceders. And it is a difficult and intricate business even to trace their history. But there can be no doubt that all these bodies exercised a powerful influence on the age to which they belonged; and there is no accounting for that but in this way, that, as it has been expressed, they 'preached *savoury* doctrine.' In other words, they were intensely and earnestly evangelical, and had power to attract and tell upon the people in a manner which the coldness and culture of Moderatism could not imitate.

7. **Evangelical Literature.**—It is also to be remembered, that if

the eighteenth century produced the histories of Robertson, the rhetoric of Blair, and the philosophy of Reid, it also produced works which had a far wider effect upon the generation than these. Not to speak of Boston, Willison, and M'Laurin, who never left the Church, there were among the Seceders men whose writings were at one time to be found in the house of almost every Scottish cottar. Among these were the *Sermons* of Ralph Erskine and *The Scots Worthies* of Howie of Lochgoin. The first of the many editions through which the latter work has passed was published in 1757, just when Moderatism had culminated; and that it must have helped to intensify the popular dislike for Robertson's policy, will be readily admitted by all who know its character.

8. **Praying Societies.**—Perhaps, however, in trying to account for the rapid increase of the Secession, we too much lose sight of an institution which originated in prelatic times, and survived the Revolution. We refer to what were called the *Praying Societies*. These societies are to be distinguished from the 'Society Men,' who were Cameronians and Nonconformists. They consisted (at least to begin with) simply of godly people, scattered over the country, who met together from time to time for their mutual edification. What good they did in keeping the temple lamp burning in dark times, we can easily imagine; but we can also see how, when the country began to ring with theological disputation, these associations became the centres of a religious propagandism. The Moderate clergy did not approve of these irregular gatherings. The Evangelicals sought to regulate them, but, on the whole, they did approve of them. The only non-controversial pamphlet ever published by Mr. Hog, the leader of the Marrow Men, was addressed to one of the societies; and Ebenezer Erskine did not think it superfluous for him to prepare rules for their direction. In these circumstances it is not wonderful that the Secession had their sympathy, and was everywhere strengthened by accessions from

their ranks. Dr. M'Kelvie, indeed, gives the names of twenty-five separated congregations which originated in their meetings.

Apart from their relation to the Secession, these praying societies—scattered over the country—must have had their effect on the public sentiment of the period. It is to take a superficial view of things, to consider only the course of party politics in the Assembly. We must think, also, of the spirit of the time. But in thinking of the spirit of the time,—as represented, for example, by Hume,—we must remember likewise how his scepticism was resisted by currents of another sort breathing through the land from the Spirit of life.

9. **Moderatism at the Close of the Century.**—After Robertson's retirement, in 1780, the Church became worse and better. It was in 1786 that Dr. M'Gill of Ayr published his work on the death of Christ, and virtually avowed himself an Arian in it. The Assembly took cognizance of the production, but was easily satisfied, and he was not even rebuked. To this time also belongs our Scottish lyrist, Robert Burns, who himself adhered to what was then called the New Light School of religionists, and whose attitude there is most significantly described by his biographer, Allan Cunningham. It is enough to say that the school, alike in theory and practice, was entirely such as to meet the liberal conditions of Mr. Buckle.

And yet things were better. It would be unpardonable to forget that even among those who were 'Moderate' in their public politics, were always some devout men who in their country parishes were doing a quiet and useful work for their Master. The number of these imperceptibly increased. Dr. Hill, who succeeded Dr. Robertson in the leadership, was a theologian, and the lectures he gave at St. Andrews, though not brilliant, were sound. His influence, therefore, was on the whole good; all the more, perhaps, that his distance from the centre prevented him from *governing* too much. Besides, the leaders of an active evangelicalism had never altogether died out of any district in the Church; and it was one of the first things to show the quickening effect of that turn of the tide which marks the beginning of modern European history. The true character of Moderatism, indeed, never appeared more strikingly than it did in 1796, when the famous debate on missions took place in the General Assembly. The proposal to appoint a collection to help in propagating the gospel abroad was treated with a fine moral indignation which, in other circumstances, it would be quite entertaining to read. 'While there remains at home,' exclaimed Mr. Hamilton of Gladsmuir, the mover of the condemnatory motion, 'a single individual without the means of religious knowledge, to propagate it abroad would be improper and absurd.' 'This,' said his seconder, Dr. Carlyle, with righteous severity—'*this* is the first time I remember to have ever heard such a proposal made.' The proposal was of course negatived. Nevertheless, there were men in the Church who were not prepared to wait till the Assembly had been converted. Under the auspices of Dr. Balfour in Glasgow, and Dr. Love in Edinburgh, private missionary societies were established in both these cities, and the amount of support they received was sufficient to show that the dominion of Moderatism was shaking.

It was not itself conscious, however, of its approaching decadence, because one of its last acts before the century ended was to commit another of those stupid mistakes which have split up the Scottish Church needlessly into fragments. Among the men awakened by the din of the French Revolution was Robert Haldane of Airthry. Having been led to accept Christ for himself, he became filled with a longing desire to make Him known to others. With this in view he sold his estate, that he might proceed as a missionary to India. The intolerance of the East India Company shut that door against him, and he then turned to the neglected classes at home. If the Moderate leaders had but known the day of their visitation, they would have welcomed such a helper; and no less those who about the same time sought to carry over the border the new life that had begun to stir in England—such men as Rowland Hill and Charles Simeon. But they were no more enlightened now than they had been when the Erskines were driven into exile. In 1799 they passed an Act which, among other things, prohibited all ministers of the Establishment 'from employing to preach, upon any occasion, or dispense any of the ordinances of the gospel,' persons not qualified to accept a presentation; and also 'from holding ministerial communion with such persons.'

The Act made the Church of Scotland a sect, and shut it out from all intercommunion, on equal terms, with the catholic world. But it served its purpose. It shut Simeon and Hill and Haldane out of all Established places of worship, and that was what was wanted. It did a great deal more than that, however. It drove another band of faithful men into Secession. The Haldanes were loyal sons of the Church, and had no thought whatever of any ecclesiastical action. What they desired was room and opportunity to preach the gospel. To get these they reared *tabernacles* here and there,—the very name indicating the temporary character of the resource. But we all know how the little spark developes into the great conflagration. The exigencies of their position brought them into contact with England, and a new form of Church government, and we have Moderatism to thank for the various forms of Scottish *Congregationalism*.

1. *When did the Moderate era begin?*
2. *Why may that date be fixed on?*
3. *Describe the character of Principal Robertson.*
4. *To what evils did his policy lead in vacant parishes?*
5. *Was his severity displayed all round?*
6. *In what did he show his laxity?*
7. *Who was the great preacher of the time?*
8. *What was the character of the preaching?*
9. *Did other causes operate to make the age?*
10. *What were they?*
11. *Name some of the influential writers of the period, and their books.*

12. How did the doctrinal teaching in the Church tell upon the Secession?
13. What famous evangelical books date from this age?
14. Give the history of the praying societies.
15. Did Moderatism grow worse or better towards the close of the century?
16. What notable event took place in the Assembly of 1796?
17. To what Act do we owe the existence of Scottish Congregationalism?

CHAPTER XI.

THE EVANGELICAL REVIVAL.

THE late Professor Islay Burns, in a work which has not been sufficiently appreciated,—*The Pastor of Kilsyth,*—describes in so graphic a way the dawn of the new time, which began with the present century, that we cannot possibly do better than quote his words:—

'It was,' says he, 'the expiring of one age and the birth of another—like that mysterious change which takes place in each diurnal round during that solemn interval between the night and the morning which all watchers in sick-chambers know so well. "Everybody," says a singularly striking and suggestive writer, "everybody at least who has watched by a sick-bed, knows that days have their appointed times, and die as well as men. There is one awful minute in the twenty-four hours when the day palpably expires; and then there is a reach of utter vacancy, of coldness and darkness; and then a new day is born, and earth restored throbs again." . . . If there is anything fanciful as regards the death and birth of days, it holds true unquestionably in regard to the death and birth of those epoch days which are the true days of the world. There are moments when the whole frame of things in the sphere of man's higher life seems "decaying and waxing old, and ready to vanish away," and then again it awakens and starts forward with a bound to a new stage of its destined race.

'In the present case the critical moment, "the awful minute" of pause and transition between life and death, lay probably somewhere between the ninetieth and the last year of the century

—nearer, perhaps, to the former than to the latter. At the beginning of that decade the night was at its very depth of chilliness and utter gloom; before it closed, the morning breath had swept over the world.

'During the same interval, too, there passed away most of those faithful witnesses who, during the latter half of the century, had maintained the standard of the truth in evil days, as if washed down by the refluent tide of the expiring age to which they belonged and in which their generation work was done. John Wesley died in 1791; Bishop Horne in 1792; John Berridge in 1793; William Romaine in 1792; Henry Venn in 1797; William Cowper in 1800,—as if entering one by one on their rest either at early dawn or break of day. John Newton lingers a little while behind, as a connecting link between the old generation and the new; but in seven years more he, too, is summoned home.

'Meanwhile another band of like brave spirits has been coming forward in their place to fight the same battle amid more stirring scenes and in a wider and more conspicuous sphere. The tide quickly turns. Evangelism, hitherto an obscure and scouted sect, skulking in byways and in corners, and confined almost exclusively to the lower orders of social life, climbs upward, and vindicates for itself a place in the highest circles and most influential spheres in the land.

'By the opening of the century the morning had fairly dawned. In the State, Wilberforce is in the very zenith of his influence and his fame. In the Church, Charles Simeon has fought fairly through his first struggles at Cambridge, and has nobly maintained his ground. Meanwhile, in an humbler sphere, the brave Rowland Hill pursues rejoicingly his evangelistic work in Surrey Chapel; and the Haldanes, with their "good news," traverse the length and breadth of Scotland; while far away in the distant East, William Carey and Claudius Buchanan, the leaders of a noble band, are already in the thick of battle on the high places of the heathen field. In 1797 the *Practical View of Christianity* was published.

In 1799 the Church Missionary Society was instituted. Other kindred institutions had either preceded it by a few years or speedily followed. As time drew on, the morning grew and grew. In 1805, Henry Martyn sailed for India. In 1806 the Slave Trade Abolition Bill was passed. In 1811 the tongue of Thomas Chalmers was first unloosed to preach the truth. In 1817 the *Astronomical Discourses* were published, and ran a race of popular favour and rapid circulation with the *Tales of my Landlord*. Meanwhile, the friends of evangelical religion multiply everywhere ; faithful ministers increase ; books of serious piety, with or without the charm of genius, are published and eagerly bought up and circulated ; Leigh Richmond's tracts, Bickersteth's treatises, the Olney hymns, and Foster's essays have each their mission and their work, and travel hither and thither in thousands over the land ; the tone of religious and moral feeling throughout society at large sensibly rises, and everything seems to presage the speedy advent of a day of spiritual life and refreshing, such as had not been seen for two hundred years.'

1. **Impatience of Pluralities.**—In the Scottish Church the spirit of the new time first showed itself in an impatience of those convenient arrangements whereby the prominent men among the Moderates attempted to monopolize as many as possible of the public offices. Scarcely had the century begun when a battle took place over a vacancy in the Edinburgh University. Dr. Macknight wished to be Professor of Mathematics as well as minister of a parish, and the leaders of his party saw no harm in the conjunction. But there had been silently growing up in the Church higher views of the functions of the Christian ministry ; and though pluralities themselves did not receive their *coup de grace* for a good many years after, there was now displayed a very keen dislike to this particular plurality. Dr. Macknight was therefore defeated. And the triumph of Sir John Leslie (with the help of the Evangelicals) was hailed as a hopeful sign of the times.

2. **Dr. Andrew Thomson.**—But the reforming element appeared in unmistakable force when *Dr. Andrew Thomson* became minister of New Greyfriars Parish, Edinburgh. He had been ordained in 1802 at Sprouston. He was translated in 1806 to Perth. And in 1810 he was transferred to the metropolis. What he at once became there may be inferred from the fact that when St. George's was opened,—the cathedral of the communion, as it was evidently intended to be,—the man who was thought worthiest to be its first minister was Dr. Thomson. His induction to this, his last charge, took place in 1814. From that date a torch was lifted up in Scotland before which the Moderatism of the Church steadily waned.

'Religion,' says Mr. Maclagan in his interesting *History of St. George's*, 'was not in disrepute at the time of Dr. Thomson's appointment. . . . Some earnestness there was in connection with one or two congregations which had recently obtained ministers of evangelical belief, faithful gospel preaching, and consistent Christian walk and conversation. But the general atmosphere was extremely worldly, cold, and indifferent; and church-going, as a rule, was attended to very much because it was generally considered a proper thing to be done. . . . But the preaching of Dr. Thomson was like a bombshell falling among the people. Not only did he give constant prominence to the distinctive gospel doctrines of grace and redemption by an atonement, but in terms of great directness and plainness of speech he denounced the customs of a society calling itself Christian; and in a marvellously short time, by his zeal and faithfulness under God, a remarkable change was effected in the habits and pursuits of many of his people.'

One of Dr. Thomson's first enterprises in the general interests of ǀEvangelicalism was the establishment of *The Christian Instructor*. That remarkable publication, which did for the new cause in Scotland what *The Tracts for the Times* did for the Oxford movement, commenced its career in August 1810, and at once became a centre round which there rallied all who desired to see the Church return to the old lines of the Reformation and the Covenants. Its early numbers are tame enough. From the kind of 'Religious Intelligence' which it reports, one can see very plainly the lie of its sympathies. It was always heartily in favour of Bible societies and missions, and that comparatively novel institution the Sabbath school. But as the currents quickened, it grew bolder and more pronounced, until its trenchant advocacy of evangelicalism provoked a vote of censure from the Moderate majority in the General Assembly itself.

3. **Thomas M'Crie and Dr. Cook.**—Another sign of the changing time appeared in the new direction which was given to the literary tastes of the clergy. The rising hope of the dominant party was Dr. George Cook, then of Laurencekirk. Like Dr. Robertson, he devoted himself to history; but, unlike him, he chose ecclesiastical subjects for investigation, and in 1811 published a work on the Reformation. A few months later there appeared a very much more famous book in the same line, M'Crie's *Life of John Knox*. And these two productions, as they indicated an already existing inclination on the part of the age to look back, so they helped to intensify the tendency to do so.

M'Crie and Cook fairly represented the two streams which can always be more or less distinctly traced through the whole of Scottish Church history; and the *Instructor*, though a Church magazine, instantly claimed kinship with the former. M'Crie was a Seceder, but he was in hearty sympathy with the Reformers. Cook was a Churchman, but (it was observed) 'he maintains uncommon reserve concerning the particular doctrines of the Reformers,' and is 'evidently perplexed on what ground to pronounce Patrick Hamilton a martyr for the truth' at all. Thus a fresh illustration was given of Hill Burton's shrewd remark in regard to the difference ecclesiastically between England and Scotland : 'The great Establishment of England,' he said, 'kept to its principles, while the Dissenters struck out innovations. On the other hand, Scottish Dissent always tended to preserve the old principles of the Church; whence the Establishment, by the progress of enlightenment, as some said,—by deterioration, according to others,—was lapsing.' Dr. Andrew Thomson recognised 'the succession' of the ancient Church rather in the Seceder than in the Moderate parish minister.

The body to which Dr. M'Crie belonged was a very small one, with an almost tragic history. It formed part of the Erskine Secession in 1732, and a part also of the Anti-Burgher Synod which was constituted on the occasion of 'the Breach' in 1749. But it set up for itself in 1806, when a document called the *Narrative and Testimony* was sought to be imposed upon its ministers as a term of communion. This document was understood by four men — M'Crie, Hog, Bruce, and Aitken — as embodying the principles of Voluntaryism. They would have had no objection to remain where they were, if they had been permitted to dissent, and if the matter had been allowed to rest as one of forbearance. But no toleration was extended to them, and they were making preparations to secede when the majority took the thing into their own hands, and pronounced a summary sentence upon them of deposition. The result was the formation of 'The Constitutional Associate Presbytery,' which developed in time into the Synod of Original Seceders. This body, after doing some admirable service, joined the Free Church in 1852, headed by a son of M'Crie, who inherited his father's tastes, and contributed materially in his day to increase the popular interest in Scottish Church history.

4. **Conversion of Chalmers.**—A far more important event, however, than any that has yet been mentioned in the present connection, was the conversion of Dr. Chalmers. He had been ordained in 1803 at Kilmany, but he was then a Moderate, with all the characteristic attributes of the order. He had no real understanding of the message which, as a minister of the gospel, he had been commissioned to deliver. He had no adequate

conception of the dignity or difficulty of his office. And as there seemed to him then no incongruity in his being at one and the same time a Professor of Mathematics in St. Andrews and the pastor of a country parish a good many miles away, so he never hesitated to let it be seen that his heart went with his philosophical rather than with his theological pursuits. The crisis of his life came when, on the 24th of December 1810, he began to read Wilberforce's *Practical View of Christianity.* 'As I got on in reading it,' he says, 'I felt myself on the eve of a great revolution in all my opinions about Christianity.' Many things had prepared him to receive the light—a long illness, family bereavements, lines of study which he had been providentially led to pursue, and other things. But through all the Spirit of God was guiding him; and when at last he rose above the mists, he soon compelled the country to recognise his mission as that of the great religious leader of his age.

God can bestow no greater common gift on a cause than that of a man of genius and eloquence to advocate it. The success of the Reformation was secured when Knox arose. And in like manner the triumphant issue of the evangelical revival might have been foretold, when first Andrew Thomson and then Thomas Chalmers appeared as its champions.

What Chalmers did in the interest of evangelical religion is matter of notoriety. Removed to Glasgow in 1814, he made the pulpit which he filled in the Tron and St. John's a living power. Then, in his more private parochial efforts, he not only directly redeemed from the wilderness some of the waste places around him, but inaugurated a new home missionary era for the entire Church. In 1823 he was translated to St. Andrews to fill the chair of Moral Philosophy; but he did not thereupon sink into the mere abstract academic lecturer. The fire which had been kindled in his heart burnt everywhere. Philosophy itself assumed a new life in his hands, and, under the impulse received through his week-day and Sabbath teaching, there sprang up a band of missionaries, some of whose names (such as that of Duff) will never be forgotten. A wider and freer field, however, opened to him, when, in 1828, he was transferred to Edinburgh, and was permitted to give himself up to the direct teaching of theology. It might truly be said that when this vantage ground was assigned to him, the cause of Moderatism was lost. To the leader of the Evangelicals was now committed the training of the future ministry of the Church; and when one thinks of the quality of his teaching and the energy and fervour with which it was given, one ceases to wonder at the rapid progress of the party he represented, and at the stand it was able to make when its hour of trial arrived.

5. **A Foreign Mission resolved on.**—A striking sign of the rise of the tide appeared in 1824, when, by a unanimous vote, the General Assembly pronounced a virtual sentence of condemnation on the anti-mission resolutions of 1796. Let us do the Moderates justice here. The motion to appoint a committee to prepare a Foreign Mission Scheme for the Church was made by Dr. Inglis, who was at the time the Moderate leader. Dr. Inglis was respected by all parties. He is said to have been an evangelical preacher, although in his public politics he led the opposite side; and his personal devoutness was acknowledged by all who knew him. But when his moving on this occasion is used for the purpose of proving that Moderatism is a maligned system, and that, for example, we owe to it that the Church of Scotland became a missionary Church, it is only fair to tell that a pretty long debate took place in the General Assembly before the conclusion he sought was unanimously come to. Dr. Inglis did indeed propose that the Church should turn its face toward heathendom, but at the same time he, at great length, endeavoured to show that *civilisation must precede Christianity;* and Dr. Duncan of Ruthwell, who followed him, explained that he would not have obtruded himself on the attention of the House 'could he otherwise have prevented his approbation of the *measure* proposed by the reverend mover from being interpreted

into an approbation of the sentiments with which the measure was introduced.'

It was a fortunate circumstance that a Moderate was moved to lead in this matter. It secured an earlier unanimity than would have been possible if the subject had been introduced by Thomson or Chalmers. But it will be remembered that the Evangelicals had not waited for the General Assembly to come to a better mind before throwing themselves into the work. Before the eighteenth century ended, they had formed societies having in view the very same objects which the Church, as such, was now contemplating in 1824; and although Dr. Duff was the first missionary who went out to India with a commission from the General Assembly, he was by no means the first minister of the Church of Scotland who had been found willing to 'hazard his life in the high places of the field.' Under the guidance of Dr. Love, the Glasgow society had been doing noble service for a quarter of a century in Africa; and when Duff landed in India in 1830, he found he had been preceded thither by such men as James Mitchell, Robert Nesbit, and John Wilson. The Evangelicals may have shown some want of faith in not earlier assuming that, though a minority, they might get the Assembly to concur with them in establishing a Church Mission. But it is a little unreasonable to claim any credit for a dominant system which positively refused to look at its obligations in 1796, which compelled so many to betake themselves to extra-mural and independent efforts, and which did not till 1824 begin even to consider the question of whether the Church ought to make an effort to 'civilise' the heathen.

6. **Dissatisfaction with Patronage.**—In so stirring a time it was impossible for thoughtful men to overlook the inconveniences which were experienced at home through the maladjustment of the civil and spiritual elements within the Church. With the evangelical revival there sprang up again the old dissatisfaction with the manner in which ministers were appointed to charges,

and the very same year which saw the Assembly resolving to engage in the missionary enterprise, saw the formation of a society having for its object 'the improving of the system of Church patronage.'

A notice announcing the public' meeting at which the society was constituted appears in *The Christian Instructor* for November 1824. It begins thus : ' It has long been an object of earnest desire among persons concerned for the advancement of the best interests of the Church of Scotland, to secure more generally the appointment of ACCEPTABLE MINISTERS to parishes. The subject has indeed been in a great measure neglected for many years, but it has never been altogether lost sight of, and recently it has attracted renewed attention ; partly from a growing impression of the deep importance of an efficient parochial clergy, and partly from the character of several appointments which have been felt as injurious to the Church.' It was now proposed, the notice went on to say, to raise funds for the purchase of such patronages as might be offered for sale, with the view of transferring them to the people directly interested.

In the same number of the *Instructor* which contains this notice, there is a significant letter which shows that besides lay patronage there was another Church difficulty coming into view. ' The evil [of patronage],' says the writer, ' is of enormous magnitude. It has worked itself into our system, and has in some measure become identified with it. Our Churchmen, too (I mean as a body), have long ceased to remonstrate against it ; and the people, when thwarted, seek other communions. The nation, then, must be aroused. . . . A better day is now dawning. Long have we slumbered, long have we slept, in all the pomp of our civil Establishment, while in our fields other sects have been reaping a plenteous harvest. . . . Is any insensible to the convulsions which patronage has caused in the Church by driving from it thousands and hundreds of thousands ? Nay, *what is more, in the partial remedy which has been applied, viz. Chapels of Ease, who sees not that one distinguishing feature of Presby-*

terianism, a parity of pastors, has been so far destroyed by introducing a kind of inferior clergy who are denied (certainly most unjustly) any share in the government of the Church.'
The meeting at which this new agitation against patronage began was held in Edinburgh on the 24th of December 1824. It was presided over by Mr. Houison Crauford of Craufordland, and among those who took part in it were Mr. Lyon of Glenogil, Sir George Sinclair, Dr. David Dickson, Dr. Henry Grey, the Rev. Walter Tait, and Dr. Andrew Thomson. The movement was a thoroughly well-intentioned one, but we have only to glance through the speeches delivered at its start to see how utterly inadequate it was to provide a remedy for the then existing state of things. 'I should delight to witness,' said Mr. Lyon, 'patronages purchased by the people themselves. They might then exultingly point to their minister and say : That is our clergyman—we have purchased him with a penny a week. They would have a feeling of property in their minister ; he would be considered by them as more their own than if merely sent among them by another.'

These good men had wakened up to the apprehension of great and pressing evils; and they were feeling after something that might promise relief. But this method of purchasing the patronages in detail was soon seen to be totally insufficient to meet the emergency, and they were driven on to face the fundamental question of whether the Church could have or had divested itself of its powers to carry out, in connection with the formation of the pastoral tie, its own essential principles.

7. **Church Extension.**—It was not till 1828 that the General Assembly formally recognised the necessity of facing on a large scale the business of Church extension. Chapels of Ease had been erected in many places where the demand for them was clamant. But not till the year named was the spiritual condition of the country at large realized in such a way as to impel to

public and united action. There can be no question that the movement which now began was another result of the evangelical revival, but it was Dr. Cook who actually made the proposal which set the Church in motion. It is curious, however, to note how helpless the Assembly felt itself to be at this stage, apart from the secular arm. What was asked was the appointment of a committee 'to collect information, to represent the evils resulting from want of church accommodation in large towns, manufacturing villages, and populous parishes, *and without delay to take the best means for bringing the matter before the notice of His Majesty's Government.*'

The committee was appointed, with Dr. Brunton as convener; but in his hands it does not appear to have achieved a great deal, and the serious agitation for the extension of the Church may be said to have only begun in 1834, when Chalmers was named convener, and threw himself into the work with an enthusiasm which set the whole country on fire. The story of this movement is rather a sad one, though very important practical lessons were learnt from it. It was assumed that the Church could not extend itself without parliamentary help, and weary years were spent in the endeavour to induce successive Governments to bestow upon it fresh endowments. But all was in vain. The journals of Dr. Buchanan show how good men broke their hearts, hanging helplessly about the purlieus of Downing Street. The Whigs refused, in the end, to give on any terms. The Tories would have endowed, but they would at the same time have enslaved, and such a condition was scornfully rejected. At last those who were thus humiliating themselves by seeking sympathy in quarters where there was none, bethought them of the mine of wealth that lay at their doors in the Christian liberality of their own people. To this Chalmers addressed himself, and was astonished at the result. Within less than seven years a sum of over £300,000 was contributed for his scheme, and an addition made of 220 churches to the number of parochial places of worship in Scotland.

8. **Controversies.**—It cannot be said, however, that the history of these days is simply the history of an advancing tide, bringing blessings with it at every step. At various times the country was convulsed with controversies, in which the combatants were not Evangelicals and Moderates, but Evangelicals and Evangelicals. The earliest of these was that which split the Bible Society into two—the bone of contention being the Apocrypha. That Andrew Thomson was right in this connection, will now be generally conceded. No Protestant society now insists on circulating the Book of Tobit. But it is equally certain that he fought the battle with a fierceness which was not always called for, and that he thus occasionally wounded friends who had as deep a love for the word of God as himself.

Another painful episode of the period is that which issued in the excision of Campbell of Row, Edward Irving, and others for heresy. Very different views have been taken of these processes, and no one who has looked carefully into them will refuse to allow that something can be said on both sides. But, after a very patient investigation of all the facts, we have no hesitation in expressing our own individual conviction that the Church, in the circumstances, was rightly guided. It is not enough to take up one isolated doctrine, and say of it that it ought to have been tenderly dealt with because it leaned to virtue's side,—was, in fact, 'only the struggle of a loving believer to find that his Redeemer was in all points tempted like as we are, yet without sin.' What the Church had to face was a powerful movement, the drift of which was indicated by the particular heresies which came to the surface ; and it showed, as events proved afterwards, a wise insight into things when it refused to look lightly upon what might seem to some trifling in itself, but which was really serious enough when viewed in the light of a symptom. The real truth we believe to be this : The Campbell-Irving movement was a pseudo-evangelical movement. At its start, it put forward such claims to spirituality, and looked so attractive, that some of the best people in the country were led away by it. But we see what it developed into—Mauricianism on the one hand, and Ritualism on the other. And we can guess what would have been the issue in the Church of Scotland if it had received house-room, and been allowed to spread. Perhaps it ought to be better known that Campbell would not have been deposed if one of the judges of the Court of Session, who happened to be a member, had not assured the Assembly that only thus could he be legally separated from his charge.

Yet another conflict came on later. It was the Voluntary controversy, in which the unexpected spectacle was exhibited of the descendants of the Erskines contending with their natural allies, the Evangelicals, over the question of the relations of Church and State. We say, 'contending with the Evangelicals,' because it is an indisputable fact that the burden of the battle fell not on the Moderates, but on Chalmers and his friends. It was a hotly-contested fight, and in the course of it words were spoken on both sides which their utterers would in after times have gladly recalled; but the controversy did good in various respects, and the bitterness of it is long since forgotten.

What was specially brought out in connection with it was the radical change which had taken place in the attitude of the Seceders toward the Established Church. They were, in fact, no longer Seceders looking forward to a possible return. They had become Dissenters, and looked on all State endowments of religion as *per se* unscriptural. It was no light matter for Scotland when this new position was taken up. In 1820 the two chief nonconforming bodies had coalesced, under the name of *The United Secession Church*, and they now constituted an organization which was formidable in many ways. It had notably grown in numbers and in self-confidence; its leading men (some of them men of remarkable ability) were taking conspicuous places on public platforms; and the lie of its sympathies being Liberal, in contradistinction to the Church, which was Tory, it acquired an influence with one of the great political parties in the State which made it impossible for any Government to ignore its opinions or opposition. We may think as we like of Voluntaryism as a principle, but no man with any observation can fail to see that here at least was the Nemesis of Moderatism. It had driven multitudes out of the Church, and had looked on contemptuously or indifferently while outlying Presbyterian sects were rising up around it in the wilderness. And now came its reward. The new atmosphere developed new ideas. And the Separatists, who were formerly either despised as powerless or patronized as possible humble helps, grew into open and formidable adversaries, whose reconciliation to the Establishment had become impossible.

1. *Mention some of the signs of a new era.*
2. *On what point in the beginning of the century did Moderatism and Evangelicalism come into collision?*
3. *Who lifted first the evangelical standard in the new century?*
4. *What periodical was greatly helpful?*
5. *Give some account of another great leader who rose at this time.*
6. *Indicate a change of attitude in the Assembly of 1824.*
7. *What new movement began in the same year?*
8. *When did the Church extension agitation begin?*
9. *State the experience of the Church in that connection.*
10. *Who led in this movement?*
11. *Name the controversies of this period.*
12. *Give some account of the merits of each.*

CHAPTER XII.

CONFLICT AND DISRUPTION.

WE have seen that so early as 1824 a society was formed to secure some relief from the pressure of patronage. It is not true, therefore, as has sometimes been affirmed, that the popular movement in the Church had its origin in the political agitation which preceded the passing of the Reform Bill, or in the exigencies created by the Voluntary controversy. Patronage was always opposed to the genius of the Scottish people, and it was inevitable that an active dislike to it should arise whenever there came to be a revival of evangelical religion. At the same time, there is no denying that the electric state of the time had much to do with the quickening of the popular discontent, and was one of the causes which moved the General Assembly in 1834 to pass the Veto Act. The Reform Bill became law in 1832. The Scotch, in the main, had taken a deep interest in its passing; and so shrewd a people could scarcely help asking why, when the political franchise had been extended, the ecclesiastical franchise should not also be liberalized.

Dr. Chalmers frankly explained, in a pamphlet published in 1840, what led him to think of the Veto. 'I was summoned,' he says, 'to attend a meeting of clergymen and elders previous by a few days to the Assembly of 1833. By this time there was a great demand in the country and throughout the Church for a mitigation of the law of patronage, and for a check on the absolute will of patrons, which had become greatly more paramount than was at all suited to the original design and genius of Presbytery. Year after year the Assembly had been plied with petitions, all of them for some change in the actual system, and many of them tending to the abolition of patronage altogether. Perhaps this general desire to popularize our ecclesiastical institutions had become all the more urgent in consequence of the movement which took place in the same direction a year or two before in the political constitution of the country. And nothing is more likely than that the new dangers which thickened around the Establishment, not by the increase of Dissenters, but by the change which had come over their spirits, had led many of the Church's friends to seek for the means of her greater safety in a greater hold on the affections of the people, and to suggest, as the likeliest method of attaching them more to the Church of their fathers, that they should recur to those ancient principles which, in the days of their fathers, were held in greater observation and honour, and which, after all, were the purest and most prosperous days of the Church of Scotland. From these and other causes there arose a very general impression that something should be done; and it was at a preliminary meeting, where I happened to be one of the number, that the Veto Act was first proposed as a method for giving effect to the will of the people, and with the least possible encroachment on the will of the patron.'

That something behoved to be done was conceded on all hands. Even Dr. Cook went so far as to propose that the people of a vacant parish should be allowed to state their reasons why they objected to any presentee offered to them, and that the presbytery should be authorized to refuse to induct him if they reckoned these reasons sufficient to justify their opposition.

The unworkableness of that plan was foreseen long before it was applied. It was applied afterwards under the Aberdeen Act, and its utter inefficacy was demonstrated. The Evangelicals held that '*unacceptableness*' for any cause was a reasonable objection *in limine;* and they set themselves to devise a scheme under which, while the existing order of things was undisturbed, the will of the people might be recognised, as of old, as a potential element in all settlements.

1. **A Turning-point in the History.**—It may be said of the 'Veto,' that of all the plans promising to be in the least effectual, it was the one which looked most rational and moderate. The CALL had been allowed to fall aside, but it had still its legal place in the Church's constitution. It was really as unwarrantable under the law to ignore the mind of the people, as it would have been to ignore the presentation of a patron. The Assembly, therefore, would not have gone beyond its powers, if it had directed that no ordination should proceed where a majority of the communicants had refused to CALL. This, however, was not proposed. An arrangement very much more favourable to patronage was agreed to—viz. that an arrest should be made on a presbytery's procedure only when a majority of the male heads of families, being communicants, came forward and formally *objected* to an induction. This was what was carried, on the motion of Lord Moncreiff, in the Assembly of 1834—a memorable era, for it was then that the tide which had been long rising fairly turned, and that the dominant place in the Church passed from the Moderates to the Evangelicals.

The step was not taken without the most serious consideration and consultation; and for a time afterwards the course of the Church was one of growing and remarkable prosperity. Between 1834 and 1838 its contributions to foreign missions trebled. In 1836 it established a colonial scheme. In 1838 Dr. Keith, Mr. M'Cheyne, Dr. Andrew Bonar, and Dr. Black were sent out to the East to seek for a suitable station in which to commence a mission to Israel, and a mission was begun in the following year. Other interests flourished in a like manner; a marked revival of spiritual religion took place all over the country, and the quickening culminated in great awakenings in Dundee and elsewhere.

2. **What the Battle was about.**—But so early as October 1834 the little cloud appeared which was destined to fill the sky with gloom. Mr. Robert Young was presented to Auchterarder, and although his call was signed by only three persons, and his settlement was opposed by 287 heads of families, he refused to see in the facts a reason why he should retire. The presbytery objected to go farther, and he appealed to the civil courts for power to compel them to do so.

Then there came to be raised quite a debateable question; that, namely, of the legality of the Veto Act. Had the Church, through its supreme court, any right to take the step it did to secure to the people a potential voice in the choosing of their ministers? Theoretically (it was supposed) the Church and the State were two independent institutions, which, for their mutual advantage, had entered into a contract, and there was no cause for any surprise being felt when a difference of opinion arose as to the terms of that contract. When Mr. Young claimed, therefore, that under the contract the presbytery was bound to take him on trial, and if they found him qualified, to induct him in the face of the people's opposition, the Church had no option but to follow him into the courts, with the view of ascertaining whether that was really the view which the State on its part took of the nature of the common bargain. It did not itself take that view. It earnestly protested against any such doctrine as that 'intrusion' had, with its consent, been made a principle of the Church. But, recognising the point as debateable, it employed advocates to show to the civil authorities that neither on the one side nor on the other had the contract ever contemplated the making of such an arrangement.

While the inquiry, however, was proceeding upon this perfectly legitimate line, claims began to be put forward on behalf of the State which startled the Church from its dream of security. One after another of the civil judges declared that the contract was a fiction—that the Church as such had no original or independent jurisdiction, and that in all causes, civil and ecclesiastical, the Court of Session and the House of Lords were supreme.

'That our Saviour,' said the Lord President, 'is the Head of the Kirk of Scotland, in any temporal, or legislative, or judicial sense, is a position which I can dignify by no other name than absurdity. The PARLIAMENT is the temporal head of the Church, from whose acts, and from whose acts alone, it exists as the National Church, and *from which alone it derives all its powers.*'

What this meant was illustrated in a series of acts which showed with unmistakable plainness on what terms alone the Scottish people were to have the benefit of a national Establishment.

(1.) The civil courts intimated that the passing of the Veto Act was *ultra vires* of the Assembly; and on the principles which they laid down in saying so, they would have pronounced equally invalid any other arrangement whatever under which the voice of the people was made potential in vacant congregations.

(2.) The Presbytery of Auchterarder was ordered, under a threat of heavy pecuniary damages, to take Mr. Young on trial, and if they were satisfied with his life and doctrine, to induct him in defiance of the popular opposition.

(3.) In the case of Lethendy a still more high-handed course was pursued. The presbytery of the bounds had presumed to ordain a minister to a purely spiritual cure there, and for this they were summoned to appear at the bar of the Court of Session, and told that nothing but the generous leniency of the judges stood in the way of their being sent to prison.

(4.) At Strathbogie a very different experience was encountered. There the court met an order of entirely subservient Presbyters. These men were prepared to do anything whatever that the civil law required. The General Assembly itself interposed to prevent them intruding a presentee into Marnoch in the face of the whole people of that parish, but its monitions were treated with contempt. For contumacy of the most daring kind, they were first suspended by their recognised spiritual superiors and then deposed, but the civil judges ordered them to continue to exercise their spiritual functions notwithstanding; and the strange spectacle was witnessed of ministers who in the eye of their Church were for the time being simply laymen, administering the most sacred ordinances under secular sanction alone.

(5.) In the same connection the judges did a yet more extraordinary thing. They drew a cordon round a particular district, and proclaimed that no man was to be allowed to preach in it except those whose commission was countersigned by themselves.

(6.) Finally, as they claimed the right to annul spiritual sentences, so they took it upon them to decide *for the Church* as well as for themselves, who alone had a title to sit in ecclesiastical courts.—Having laid down the law on that point, they proceeded to revise, as it suited them, the proceedings of all presbyteries which were not constituted as they thought they should be. There was no limit to their powers of intrusion under this rule. Wherever there was a *quoad sacra* minister, his presence was held to vitiate all processes whatever, and kirk-sessions found, to their consternation, that the key of discipline was not in their hands, but in those of the sheriff.

3. **The Church's Alarm.**—The Church was confounded by this succession of assaults upon its liberties, and the outcry which it made was loud and violent. It had been proceeding with a light heart and an elastic step—like a giant refreshed by sleep— to do all the good it could for Scotland and for the world, when it was startled by finding the State, with which it was in alliance, and whose interests it was trying to serve, seizing it, as it were, by the throat, and doing its very best to pinion and paralyze it. It discovered that the Establishment, which was intended to support it, was being made very much less of a help than Saul's armour was to David. It was, in fact, proving to be not a help at all, but a set of fetters interfering on every hand with the free

exercise of its powers. If the judges were right in their interpretation of the law, then the Church of Scotland had, for the sake of its endowments, bartered away what it had no right to dispose of. Its earnest contention was that the law was not interpreted correctly, and it was supported in this view by five of the most distinguished Senators of the College of Justice. But against a preponderating judicial vote it had no legal remedy; and it asked the Legislature to interfere with a new Act to prevent the catastrophe of a Disruption. The Crown was advised at the time by a Conservative Ministry—and especially by Sir James Graham and Lord Aberdeen. The time came when both these statesmen expressed bitter regret that they had failed to apprehend the true nature of the crisis. Sir James told Dr. Buchanan that 'he would never cease to regard it as the saddest event in his life that he should have had any hand' in what he called 'a most fatal act.' But, unfortunately, they refused to listen to all warnings at the moment, and the crash came.

4. **A Disruption made inevitable.** — A disruption was made absolutely unavoidable. The only conditions on which the State was willing to maintain its alliance with the Church were these :—

(1.) That what was in effect Principal Robertson's famous law should continue to be binding, popular acceptability being set aside as not at all a *sine qua non* in the matter of a settlement.

(2.) That the Church should consent to a sacrifice of certain of her essential rights; that, for example, she should surrender her inherent title to carry out the principles of Presbyterianism, by giving to all ministers having charge of congregations the position of rulers as well as of teachers, and concede that its most spiritual sentences were to be held as invalid whenever declared to be so by the civil courts.

(3.) That, above all things, this controlling doctrine should be accepted and acted upon : that, when any difference of opinion arose between Church and State as to whether a particular matter was civil or spiritual, it should belong to the civil judges to *decide supremely for both.*

5. **A New Breach.**—The Evangelical party could not consent to continue in alliance with the State on these terms. On the 18th of May 1843 another great 'breach' occurred in the Church, and the Revolution Establishment was made a good deal less 'national' than it had been before.

Mr. Gladstone, writing in 1849 to acknowledge receipt of a copy of *The Ten Years' Conflict,* related to Dr. Robert Buchanan an interesting little anecdote, which is worth introducing here. 'A friend of mine,' he said, 'a conscientious and earnest-minded French Roman Catholic, well acquainted with our country and language, once told me that, amid his discouragements in witnessing the progress of unbelief in so many quarters, he had found a singular comfort in the testimony borne by the ministers and members of the Free Church of Scotland to the authority of conscience and of positive religious belief.'

What did take place when this new fruit of Moderate policy appeared, is described by Lord Cockburn. The 18th of May had arrived, and the General Assembly of the yet unbroken Church of Scotland had convened. 'Dr. Welsh, Professor of Church History in the University of Edinburgh, having been Moderator last year, began the proceedings by preaching a sermon before his Grace the Commissioner in the High Church, in which what was going to happen was announced and defended. The Commissioner then proceeded to St. Andrew's Church, where the Assembly was to be held. The streets, especially those near the place of meeting, were filled, not so much with the boys who usually gaze at the annual show, as by grave and well-dressed people of the middle rank. According to custom, Welsh took the chair of the Assembly. Their very first act ought to have been to constitute the Assembly of this year by electing a new Moderator. But before this was done, Welsh rose and announced that he and others who had been returned as members held this not to be a free Assembly, that, therefore, they declined to acknowledge it as a court of the Church, that they meant to leave the very place, and, as a consequence of this, to abandon the Establishment. In explanation of the grounds of this step he then read a full and clear protest. Whether from joy at the prospect of getting rid of their troublesome brethren anyhow (which they preferred), or from being alarmed (which to a great degree was the truth), the Moderate party, though they might have objected to any paper being read, even from the chair, at this time attempted no interruption, which they now regret. The protest resolved itself into this: That the civil court had subverted what had ever been understood to be the Church; that its new principles were enforced by ruinous penalties; and that in this situation they were constrained to abandon an Establishment which they felt to be repugnant to their vows and to their consciences. As soon as it was read, Dr. Welsh handed the paper to the clerk, quitted the chair, and went away. Instantly, what appeared to be the whole left side of the house rose to follow. Some applause broke from the spectators, but it checked itself in a moment. One hundred and ninety-three members moved off, of whom about one hundred and twenty-three were ministers and about seventy elders. Among these were many upon whose figures the public eye had been long accustomed to rest in reverence. . . .

'As soon as Welsh, who wore the Moderator's dress, appeared in the street, and people saw that principle had really triumphed over interest, he and his followers were received with the loudest acclamation. They walked in procession down Hanover Street to Canonmills, where they had secured an excellent hall, through an unbroken mass of cheering people and beneath innumerable handkerchiefs waving from the windows. But amidst this exultation there was much sadness and many a tear, many a grave face and fearful thought, for no one could doubt that it was with sore hearts that these ministers left the Church; and no thinking man could look on the unexampled scene and behold that the temple was rent, without pain and sad forebodings. No spectacle since the Revolution reminded one so forcibly of the Covenanters.'

'The Free Church,' Lord Cockburn goes on to say, 'is distinguished from all past or existing sects of Scotch Presbyterians in this, that its adherents are not almost entirely of the lower orders. They have already peers, baronets, and knights, provosts and sheriffs, and a long train of gentry. The Lord Provost of Edinburgh walked with them from St. Andrew's Church to Canonmills, where the late Provost of Glasgow and the Sheriff of Mid-Lothian joined them. And that extraordinary procession was dignified by about eight old Moderators, two Principals of Universities, and four Theological Professors. . . . This is the first time that our gentry are not only not ashamed of Presbytery, but not ashamed of it with the additional vulgarity of unendowed dissent. . . . In some views these self-immolations of the ministers are surpassed by the gallantry of the two hundred probationers, who have extinguished all their hopes at the very moment when the vacancies of four hundred and fifty pulpits made their rapid success almost certain. . . . What similar sacrifice has ever been made in the British Empire? . . . It is the most honourable fact for Scotland that its whole history supplies. The common sneers at the venality of our country, never just, are now absurd.'

The General Assembly of the Free Church was immediately constituted in the great Hall, to which Lord Cockburn refers, under the moderatorship of Chalmers. Around him were gathered all the men who had rendered themselves most prominent in promoting 'the evangelical revival.' Candlish, Cunningham, Guthrie, Gordon, Dunlop, Graham Spiers, etc.,— and thus a stream which might have been kept within the Establishment and preserved it, was driven forth to pursue an independent course to its inevitable detriment.

6. **The Remanent Assembly.**—Meanwhile the Assembly which

had been abandoned addressed itself to the work which lay to its hand to do, and from the course which it pursued we have no difficulty in apprehending the historical significance of the event which had occurred. The Church, relieved of the evangelical element, went back at once to the *status quo ante bellum*. The Moderate party had succeeded with the help of the secular arm in driving its natural opponents out of the field, and with its return to power came a frank replacement of its party policy.

First, the Veto Act having been declared by the civil courts to be illegal, that is, to have been passed by the Church without due authority, was not repealed, but simply blotted as worthless out of the Statute Book, and all presbyteries were ordered to proceed henceforth in the settlement of parishes 'according to the practice which prevailed previously to the passing of the Act.' In other words, the intrusion of an unacceptable minister upon a reclaiming people was again recognised as a possible and a legitimate contingency.

Next, the Strathbogie ministers were declared to be ministers in good standing, notwithstanding that they had been solemnly deposed by the supreme court of the Church. Their direct right to administer the Sacraments was notoriously derived from the Court of Session alone. It was within the competency of those who were now in power to cancel the sentence which had been passed upon them by a former General Assembly, and to restore them honourably and in an orderly way to the position from which they had been driven; but that ceremony was not thought to be needed. The civil authorities had pronounced the Act of Deposition to be null and void, and Dr. Cook and his supporters revealed their historic standpoint by bowing submissively to the judgment.

Again, the principles of Presbyterian parity had been carried out in 1833, when the ministers of the parliamentary Churches were allowed to sit in Church courts; in 1834, when the chapel of ease ministers were in like manner emancipated; and in 1839, when the Old Light Burgher body joined the Establishment, and their congregations were allowed to retain all the spiritual privileges which they had enjoyed in a state of secession. But in the Stewarton case the civil judges had declared that the Church, by accepting Establishment, had denuded itself of its original power to do as it did ; and its acts being pronounced to have been 'incompetently passed,' were obsequiously, and without going through the form of repeal, swept out of the Statute Book.

In connection with all these proceedings it will be observed the ruling principle was unreservedly recognised, that when the civil court had spoken, there remained nothing for the Church to say. The Court of Session intimated that the Veto Act was incompetent, and the Church as re-established after the Disruption meekly acquiesced. The same authority had recognised the spiritual standing of the ministers of Strathbogie after their deposition, and the Church did not presume to disagree. The Senators of the College of Justice intimated that a property qualification was needed for a man to be a Presbyterian minister in full standing, and once more the obedient Assembly said *Amen.*

The judges may have been right, as a matter of fact, in the view they took of the Church's constitution as Established. Perhaps it was really the case that the Church, in accepting the support of the State, had conceded to it a power *in sacris* which was unsuspected until the great judicial decisions prior to 1843. But no evangelical Presbyterian could with any consistency assent to such a concordat as justifiable in itself ; and when the actual state of the case was disclosed, there was only one loyal course for him to take, and that was to surrender the endowments which he had been enjoying, and endeavour to fulfil his ecclesiastical mission with such other assistance as might be available. This accordingly was what was done by those who believed that for a Church to be useful it must be free.

7. **Constituent Elements.**—It would be to advance an absurd claim on behalf of the Free Church to say that it carried out with it all that was good in the Establishment. It had, to begin with, a splendid set of leaders; all over the country it was joined by the men who had been taking an active part in works of reformation; and among the many other testimonies borne to its position, it was accepted at once as the true Church of Scotland by all the missionaries who had been sent out by the unbroken Church to Jew or Gentile. But it would be folly to deny that the power of sympathy brought into its ranks many who had little understanding of its principles, and that not a few were left behind whose piety and true-heartedness were unquestionable.

In these facts lies the hope of ultimate reconciliation. The old Church is not broken up into fragments which have no affinities with one another. Each lump contains elements common to all. And when the breath of a divine life melts the masses, what is best in them all will coalesce. At the same time, there is no mistaking how the great historical Church parties for the time adjusted themselves. In the Established Church, as we see it starting again on a new career in 1843, we behold the Moderate party once more on the crown of the wave; while in the Free Church at the same date we see the Evangelicals—discomfited as it appeared—driven out of the citadel into the open, yet in the open maintaining a fight, the final issue of which still remains to be determined.

8. **Efforts at Readjustment.**—That the stage of 'finality' has not yet been reached in the Presbyterian history of Scotland is manifest; and this has been recognised in the attempts which have more than once been made since the Disruption to adjust the Establishment to its now confessedly anomalous position.

One obvious mistake, however, has appeared in all these efforts. Those who were called upon to advise the Crown have utterly failed to realize the fact that those who were driven out of the Establishment in former times by the fault of others, have a moral right to be consulted now with regard to any fresh alliance with the State.

In the last legislative effort the blundering was peculiarly conspicuous. Not only was it assumed that the only consideration to be thought of was the strengthening of the one section of the ancient Church which happens to retain possession of the endowments (which was a most unstatesmanlike idea), but the reforms proposed were at once absurdly unsuited in their own nature to the parties for whose benefit they were intended, and, in their avowed design and mode of presentation, were fitted to provoke and irritate conscientious Nonconformists instead of conciliating them.

Dr. Cook and Dr. Robertson of Ellon, who moved the acts rescissory in the first Assembly after the Disruption, were the natural successors of Principal Robertson and Dr. Hill. These leaders—the men of 1843—have passed away, and their places have been filled by others who so far differ from them that they have taken on the colour of the time. But there can be no question about this, that it is virtually the same party—the Moderate party—which is still in power. There has not been within the past generation any such new 'evangelical revival' in the Established Church as to suggest that the tide has turned. Many individual ministers are Evangelicals, just as was the case in the end of last century. But the prevailing current was still that which swept the Non-Intrusionists into the wilderness, when in 1874, the Church had offered to it the extraordinary boon of *the abolition of patronage.* The offer was a sort of anachronism. What distinguished the Moderates of old time was their dislike to popular election. For the sake of patronage they had broken up the Church and risked the Establishment. And now there seemed something absurdly grotesque in the idea that they should be rewarded for their fidelity by getting what they had fought against to the death.

Unfortunately, however, the humorous side of the transaction was not the only one which arrested attention. An irritating element was introduced into the affair by the circumstance (which there was no attempt made to conceal) that the ancient principles of the party had been sacrificed for proselytizing purposes. No effort was made to combine all the Presbyterian Churches, as such, in an endeavour to secure a new concordat from the State; but a colourable imitation was made of the banners of the nonconforming bodies in the hope of attracting individual members of these bodies into the Establishment. In other words, the idea of recognising the historical standing of the Free and United Presbyterian Churches was not entertained, but a device was resorted to with the view of breaking up these Churches by the process of gradual absorption.

A scheme like this could not but fail. Even had it been essentially perfect in all respects, it would have broken down, because of its unattractive history. But it has not been recognised as satisfactory in itself by either of the Churches most concerned. The old system of lay patronage has indeed been abolished, but what remains is not the 'right which appertains to the Christian people to elect their own ministers,' but a civil right, conferred by Act of Parliament upon a selected constituency which includes adherents as well as communicants, and whose powers are limited to a given time. Besides, the old difficulty of the two jurisdictions remains as before. It is still the case that the Church cannot, without the leave of the State, give to any Scottish minister the full presbyterial power to rule as well as teach. And the law is still unchallenged which makes the House of Lords the supreme arbiter in all causes, civil and ecclesiastical. Of course those who are satisfied with the Establishment as at present constituted have something to say for themselves. They can argue that they have universal suffrage in the Church as well as in the State, and that, as events have proved, a nonconforming body even is not safe from the encroachments of civil courts. But there is the ready reply, (1) that (apart from other things) the equal vote of an *adherent* is a novelty in church experience, and (2) that, while it is quite true even of a Free Church that it may be harassed by the secular power, that Church can always save itself from complicity in the intrusion by refusing to condone it. We are not responsible for the misconduct of another, if we protest against that misconduct. We are so far responsible when we wink at it, and accept favours on the distinct understanding that it is to be winked at. Of all safeguards against mistakes of administration in a Church, the worst practically is that of submitting its spiritual sentences to be reviewed by a civil judge. But whether that be the case or no, no Church, it is held, has any right to surrender its freedom to any power outside; and it is just as irrational to argue that because liberty of conscience is not allowed in Spain no individual should try to assert it, as it is to say of a Church that the State does not recognise its independence, and therefore it should cease to claim it.

9. **The Scottish Churches.**—In 1847 the United Secession and Relief Churches joined, and took the name of the United Presbyterian Church. This is now a powerful and well-compacted body, with nearly 180,000 communicants. It has a good hold on all the great centres of population, and is notably vigorous in the carrying on of missionary operations abroad.

The Free Church, which started with 470 ministers, has now 1050, with as many congregations. Its communicants number about 300,000, and its income is much larger than that of any other denomination in Scotland. Its missions, too, are maintained on a great scale in India, Africa, and the New Hebrides. Two nonconforming bodies have united with it since the Disruption—the Original Seceders and the Cameronians.

The Established Church claims to have over 500,000 communicants, but it has been demonstrated that this must be an over-estimate, and that is confirmed by the census which has been taken in many parts of the country. Everywhere it is shown that while it continues to be the largest individual sect, at least in the lowlands, its worshippers are certainly far fewer in number than those of the Free and United Presbyterian Churches combined.

Besides these three bodies, which, between them, occupy the land most fully, there are many other sects. In certain districts there are to be found some remains of the indigenous Romanism of the country, rising like the roots of ancient forest trees in a modern clearing; and to these have been added, chiefly by immigration from Ireland, so many accessions that Popery is now represented in Scotland by more than 300,000 souls. Episcopacy has also gathered strength. It, too, has been largely recruited from outside—from England. In fact, though there are certain things about it which connect it in a peculiar way with our Scottish past, it bears to this day many of the marks of an English exotic. Yet it is growingly influential. A large proportion of the gentry have attached themselves to it. It is still the custom among our better classes either to send their children for education across the border, or to those schools nearer home which are conducted on English models. And now, as formerly, its ornate services, with other things, attract the young and the would-be fashionable. This is not the place to say a word about the merits or demerits of modern Episcopacy. But we may allow ourselves to give expression to the conviction that the nation's truest interests will be best conserved by a revived devotion to our national Presbyterianism.

Apart from these larger denominations, there are not a few others which, together, make up a considerable section of the population. The healing of breaches is seldom so complete as to leave no splinters behind, and though the Covenanters and Original Seceders joined the Free Church in mass, there remained outside a few congregations of each, which still profess to uphold their ancient banners. The Congregationalists, also, are in some force. The Baptists have several congregations. And there are Wesleyans and others to illustrate the almost infinite variety of religious opinion which prevails in the world.

Nor, however, must we forget to add, that beyond all the Churches lies an outfield which is filled by a teeming multitude of persons who have forsaken Christian ordinances altogether. It is possible that during the present generation there may take place another readjustment in the relations of the leading Churches. But nothing of that kind will be of the highest value if it does not issue in the reclamation of the waste places.

10. **Where is the Succession?**—It is interesting to notice in connection with the history of a Church what constitutes its 'Succession'—by what characteristic marks it can be identified from age to age. It is evident that 'Establishment' or 'Non-Establishment' is not one of these marks. From 1661 to 1689 there was a national Establishment, but the Church of Sharp and Claverhouse was not the Church of Knox and Henderson. The Church of Scotland, lying in the line of the succession, was then in the wilderness, and William of Orange recognised the fact when at the Revolution he brought the covenanting remnant to the front, and reconstituted the Establishment round them.

1. One mark was certainly *Presbyterianism*. The Reformation was achieved by Presbyters. The Presbyterian system was developed in the *First Book of Discipline*. And although, once and again, the Church assumed an Episcopal guise, the transformation was always submitted to under compulsion, and whenever the pressure was withdrawn it reverted to its original form.

2. Another mark was *evangelical teaching*. No doubt there were times when very uncertain sounds were heard from the pulpits of the Church of Scotland. But its earliest standards were evangelical—so are the Confession of Faith and its Catechisms; and although among its divines there have been not a few men like Blair and M'Gill, the national instinct has never failed to recognise 'the succession' in preachers of the type of Chalmers.

3. A third mark was *a love for spiritual liberty and independence*. But for this the Scottish people could have retained

no independent religious ideas or forms of their own. Again and again, in successive generations, they have been subjected to assaults upon their freedom—from Rome, from England, from Kings, from Parliaments, from Churchmen, from Statesmen; and it is not surprising that under this kind of training there was developed a sturdy self-reliance, which has given a distinct and perfectly recognisable colouring to the historical Church of the country. You see it wherever it asserts its right to hold its own against tyranny in any form. It disappears when there is manifested a facile disposition to submit to and be moulded by others.

4. A fourth mark was the strength of its *popular sympathies*. It held high views of the Church as a divine institution. It held equally high views of the position which was occupied by each individual member. The Moderate idea of the Christian people was that they were so many sheep for whom a shepherd behoved to be chosen. The characteristic idea of the Scottish Church is that they are citizens in a commonwealth, qualified by character and education to choose a teacher for themselves. The whole constitutional framework of Presbyterianism is democratic. Every part of the system is worked so as to call forth the energies and responsibilities of the individual; and the course of 'the succession' can be traced quite clearly in the degree of respect which the different parties paid to the voice of the people.

'*Ubi Christus, ibi Ecclesia*' is the oldest and truest Church mark in the world. We may extend it so far and say: if you want, at the present time, to find the Church of Scotland—the Church of the Reformation, and of the Covenants—the Church of Knox, and Melville, and Rutherford, and Boston, and the Erskines—you must seek it not exclusively in any one denomination, but among the membership of the various fragments into which the ancient national institute has been broken. Wherever the marks indicated appear, there will be met the life-stream which we hope and believe will yet cover the whole land.

CONFLICT AND DISRUPTION. 161

1. *How did the Veto Act come to be proposed?*
2. *What were the terms of that Act?*
3. *Did the Church prosper after it passed? if so, in what way?*
4. *What was the first question raised in the conflict?*
5. *How would you say that this question was debateable?*
6. *What new claims were started by the civil courts?*
7. *Quote the words of the Lord President.*
8. *Give illustrations of what this meant.*
9. *What power did the Court of Session claim at Auchterarder, at Lethendy, at Strathbogie?*
10. *How did the Church feel under these assaults on her liberty?*
11. *Did the State give relief?*
12. *Who were responsible for the Government at this time? and how did they come to look at things?*
13. *What were the principles at stake? Indicate them.*
14. *Why was a Disruption inevitable?*
15. *What did Lord Cockburn think of the Disruption?*
16. *What did the Established Church Assembly do after the Evangelicals had left it?*
17. *What did these Acts imply?*
18. *To what important principle did the Established Church give assent?*
19. *What historical party triumphed in* 1843?
20. *Have we now seen the last stage of Scottish history?*
21. *What efforts have been made since the Disruption to readjust things?*
22. *Have these succeeded?*
23. *If not—why not?*
24. *Describe the present condition of the several Scottish Churches.*
25. *What constitutes the Succession in any Church?*
26. *What are the leading characteristics of the Church of Scotland?*
27. *Where is now the life-stream?*

L

www.ingramcontent.com/pod-product-compliance
Lightning Source LLC
Chambersburg PA
CBHW030246170426
43202CB00009B/646